VOLUME TWO

Basics *for* Believers

Foundational Truths to Guide Your Life

William L. Thrasher, Jr.

MOODY PRESS
CHICAGO

ISBN: 0-8024-3744-3

1 3 5 7 9 10 8 6 4 2

Printed in the United States of America

To our children,
Keith and Laura Connor
Travis and Sharon Thrasher

There is no greater joy than to see your children walking in the truth and light of Scripture.

Contents

Section 3

GOD WITH US

Section 4

A GODLY LIFE

Section 5

A WATCHFUL LIFE

Section 6

AN ORGANIZED LIFE

Section 7

A DISCIPLINED LIFE

Section 8

A GOAL-ORIENTED LIFE

Foreword

If one is concerned with theological precision, it is by no means an easy task to explain Christian doctrines like the sovereignty of God, the atonement, and the doctrine of justification in simple terms that most lay people can readily follow without losing interest. That is the task Bill Thrasher has undertaken for himself in the *Basics for Believers* series. He does a superb job of it, too. He is clearly gifted with a keen mind and a solid grasp of the Christian faith—as well as an uncanny ability to present truth in a simple, fresh, and accessible way.

Concern for sound doctrine seems to be waning among evangelicals these days. Even pastors are increasingly obsessed with methodology and other pragmatic issues, and many are surprisingly ill-equipped to teach sound doctrine or even safeguard their flocks from doctrinal aberrations. But the health and future of the evangelical movement depends on our ability to hold firm doctrinally.

That's why I am so thankful for this series. It's a handy, reliable guide that will be helpful to lay people and pastors alike. It is both interesting and accurate;

the style is as simple as these truths are profound. Bill Thrasher's love of doctrine is contagious.

Basics for Believers answers a crying need for the church today. Solid teaching like this has been growing harder and harder to find for many years. My hope is that this book signals the reversal of that trend.

JOHN MACARTHUR

Acknowledgments

Of the many blessings in writing this second volume of *Basics for Believers* series, none compares with the growing knowledge and understanding of the character and perfections of the Triune God of Scripture.

I stand in awe and amazement as I sense God's sovereign rule and providential care over all the affairs of my life. I am eternally indebted to this great God for the precious gift of salvation through His Son. I thank Him for the abundant resources and opportunities to which I have been privileged. I am grateful for the special people who have placed critical roles in helping me fulfill a deep desire to proclaim to a lost and dying world the truths of Scripture about the God of Creation.

In appreciation, I begin with my life partner and best friend, Mary, who not only is my wife but also my editor, advisor, and encourager. I also thank my children, to whom I have dedicated this book, for their continued love and encouragement and the examples they set in their love of God in everyday life.

Thanks to "The Team" at Moody Press for their continued dedication, hard work, and sacrifice throughout the process of "making a book."

A special thank-you goes to Greg Thornton and

Dennis Shere, who not only have encouraged me in writing, but have inspired me by their godly character and leadership.

No book would ever be its best without the work of the editorial process. I want to thank Tracey Sumner and Anne Scherich for their talents in providing the final shaping and polishing to the finished product.

Last, I am so grateful to God for those wonderful authors, pastors, and teachers who continue to provide marvelous resources that give everyone the opportunity to learn and grow in their faith. This book would have been impossible without them. Please take time to see their names and works listed in the Appendix.

Introduction

When I wrote *Basics for Believers* (the first volume), I introduced the book by saying that life is a journey. When I wrote that, I was referring to John Bunyan's all-time best-seller *Pilgrim's Progress,* which I believe is still one of the best analogies of what a true life of faith is all about. *Pilgrim's Progress* explains how the Christian life can fulfill the purposes God has revealed to us in the Scriptures. This helps explain why it is the best-selling book, other than the Bible, of all time. Understanding and living out these same principles is what *Basics for Believers, Volume 2* is all about.

I believe there are three major barriers that hinder believers' successful fulfillment of God's purposes. First, many believers begin their journey of faith—a journey God called them to—without a clear vision of the objectives of their new life in Christ. Consequently, many are drawn into religious activities that seem OK but are not really grounded in Scripture. Others may end up in churches and denominations that are doctrinally weak or preoccupied with pursuits that are not necessarily at the core of biblical Christianity. Moreover, today most believers are not introduced to solid biblical catechism (a summary of religious doctrine, often in the form of questions and answers) with Scripture texts to help them recognize what it really means to be a believer.

The second barrier that keeps many believers from the joy of the victorious Christian life is that they fall prey to a modern heresy that says the truth of the Scriptures is not sufficient for all things in their lives. Today, we have become consumed with method instead of the content of the message. Many are convinced that we must entertain in order to engage, and that the simple approach of preaching the Word and proclaiming Christ is outdated. I am convinced that over the past century we have lost sight of some of the great truths of our faith, and two that come to mind are the understanding of the sufficiency of Scripture and the abundant power of the Holy Spirit.

Popular "self-help methods" have replaced the foundational emphasis on the truth of God's written Word and the work of the Holy Spirit when it comes to growth for the believer. There are many movements, seminars, and programs based on man's wisdom and not God's.

Another preoccupation for many who are called into the Christian faith is that of the focus on the external rather than the internal. The Scriptures consistently warn us against being attentive to the outside and missing the real need for change on the inside. True faith involves being totally honest with God and with ourselves. When we do that through the power of the Holy Spirit, we begin to realize our desperate need for change within ourselves. It is from an internal transformation that the new life of a believer begins to manifest itself on the outside.

The third hindrance is the tendency to compartmentalize our spiritual lives to only certain times on Sunday or a few other special times while living the rest of our lives the same way most unbelievers live—preoccupied with the pursuit of making a living, raising families, and finding enjoyment. In that case, God tends to be an afterthought and, for the most part, does not enter into the thoughts and plans of the day. Many believers have forgotten the importance of starting every day with God and allowing Him to order and influence our lives.

The truth is that this is not biblical Christianity. The Bible makes it clear that it is not just what we believe but also what we do in reflection of that faith that demonstrates our relationship with God.

If your life is not centered on Him, then change is imperative. It is my hope that this book will help you make needed changes in your Christian walk, as you continue to review the basics of the faith.

Section 1

GOD OF ALL

1
God's Creation

The works of the L*ORD are great, studied by all who have pleasure in them (Psalm 111:2* NKJV*).*

In early 1990, the National Aeronautics & Space Administration (NASA), in a cooperative effort with the European Space Agency, launched the Hubble Space Telescope. Hubble was designed to provide astronomers with a completely unrestricted view of the heavens. It has given mankind new insights into the universe and greatly enhanced our knowledge about the size, formation, and life cycle of the stars.

The more we learn about the heavens, the more amazing we recognize this universe to be. It is so vast we do not know where its limits are, nor does there seem to be an end to what we can learn about it.

Closer to home, the study of genetics has advanced our understanding of just how fearfully and wonderfully the human body is made, and it has helped us understand the uniqueness of each person. The discovery and study of DNA and its distinct combinations has led us to the discovery of the causes of numerous medical difficulties and how many of them may be corrected.

A little reading on these subjects alone demonstrates the magnitude of what mankind has discovered about God's creation, which causes us to stop and ponder for a moment where this all came from and how it came to be.

As believers, we know that the Bible provides the answers we need. In the first chapter of Genesis, God gives simple answers to the questions surrounding the beginning of the universe. The Bible was never meant to give us an in-depth, detailed account of the formation and history of creation. But as scientists discover more about how our universe came into existence, we can see how those discoveries line up with the truth revealed in the Bible.

As believers, we should not allow foolish theories such as evolution (which, by the way, has now been discredited by many reputable scientists) or other nonbiblical speculations concerning the formation of the universe to distract us from the revealed truth of Scripture. Nor should we be discouraged by debate among Christians as to whether we should embrace an "young earth" view of creation, which holds to the literal interpretation of six creation days, or a "old earth" view, which asserts that the "days" referred to in Scripture were actually long periods of time. God alone knows how He chose to do these things.

The study of creation is a worthwhile exercise, for in learning of creation we learn of our Creator—of His creativity and the creativity He imparts to us. As we study the creation, the marvelous wonders of God's handiwork unfold before us, and we begin to see that God provided creation to give us some understanding of the incredible wisdom of the One we call our Creator. This knowledge we gain through studying creation is called "general revelation," which is a limited knowledge of God that all humans possess.

When God finished creating the universe and the world on which we live, He said it was "good." In fact, it was perfect! God enjoyed perfect fellowship with Adam and Eve, the first humans. But sin entered the picture, bringing separation between God and humankind. As believers, we now understand that we can be reconciled to God only through Jesus Christ, who died to restore the perfect fellowship Adam and Eve enjoyed with their heavenly Father.

Now that we have fellowship with the Father through Jesus, we should strive to rediscover the awesomeness of our heavenly Father, the Creator-God, who made all we see, just to give us a sense of His majesty and grandeur. As we grow in our understanding of the doctrine of creation, our desire to know Him more and to bow before Him in worship and praise will be strengthened as well.

ACTION STEP:

Pick out a subject related to any area of creation (the cosmos, the human body, the study of our planet Earth) and do some reading from a biblical perspective. Keep in mind that the God who created all is the same God who desires fellowship with you through His Son, Jesus Christ.

FOR FURTHER READING:

The Genesis Question
chapter 1, pp. 9–12; and chapter 21, pp. 183–87
Hugh Ross

2

God's Sovereignty

Yours, O L*ORD, is the greatness, the power and the glory, the victory and the majesty; for all that is in heaven and in earth is Yours; Yours is the kingdom, O* L*ORD, and You are exalted as head over all (1 Chronicles 29:11* NKJV*).*

During the past twenty years I have become familiar with a number of Christian authors and their works. There are a special few whose writings the Holy Spirit has used to make an impact on my life of faith. One such writer was Arthur W. Pink, one of the most prolific Christian writers of the twentieth century and a man who provided a critical link to the Puritan writers.

One of Pink's more than fifty titles is his classic, *The Sovereignty of God,* first published in 1917 and still available today. I believe every Christian should read this book, especially in light of the flawed understanding and view of God among believers today. In it, Pink speaks of the Lord God Almighty as the One who possesses all power in heaven and earth and the One who is sovereign over everything.

Sadly, the word *sovereignty* is not widely used or understood today. The dictionary defines sovereignty as "a supreme power over something" and "something that is free from external control." One familiar earthly example of sovereignty is the United States Supreme Court, which has the ultimate say when it comes to the interpretation of the laws of our land. Likewise, God has supreme power over the universe, which He formed by His word. He is sovereign over everything and everyone. He maintains that sovereignty by controlling or allowing every event that has taken place or ever will take place.

But, many of us ask, if God is sovereign over all, couldn't He have stopped sin from coming into the picture? The origin of sin is one of the great mysteries of our faith. God is holy and righteous in all His ways, and He did not *create* sin. On the other hand, God *permitted* sin in order that some of His wondrous attributes might be displayed.

Scripture makes clear the doctrine of the sovereignty of God, yet it never absolves man of his responsibility. God did not cause the Fall, but He permitted it in that He gave Adam and Eve the freedom to choose sin. Adam bears full responsibility for his transgression of God's standard of obedience.

From before the beginning of time, God had full knowledge that sin would enter the world, and He had a plan to deal with this great tragedy. At the right time, God sent His Son, Jesus Christ, to pay the price for the sins of a fallen mankind.

The God of the Bible is truly sovereign and very different from the god so many serve today. Many people today—even those who claim the name "Christian"—have a manageable deity who operates according to their likes and dislikes. Their god is an idol who bows to the will of the creature. Their god is a comfortable imitation who never convicts of sin and who is not sovereign over all creation.

We should rejoice in the truth of God's sovereignty. This doctrine serves to humble us before the triune

God and motivate us to live holy and righteous lives of obedience. It also helps us to be thankful in all circumstances, as we recognize that God is sovereign over all and that He works everything for our good, because we love Him.

ACTION STEP:

Look up the words awesome *and* mighty *in a concordance; then look up the Scriptures listed and read what the Bible says about God's sovereignty.*

FOR FURTHER READING:

The Sovereignty of God
chapter 1, pp. 19–27
Arthur W. Pink

3
Providence

Do not forget the things I have done throughout history. For I am God—I alone! I am God, and there is no one else like me. Only I can tell you what is going to happen even before it happens. Everything I plan will come to pass, for I do whatever I wish (Isaiah 46:9–10).

Providence. This is a subject every believer should hold very dear. It is a subject in which to delight and one from which to draw great comfort and strength on the journey of faith.

Sadly, God's providence is for many a little-understood doctrine whose meaning and relevance to everyday life is much different from that of earlier times. However, the Bible has a lot to say about God's providence and the role it plays in every detail of a believer's life. The Bible reveals to us that providence is displayed in the entire plan of history and in the redemptive purposes accomplished through the person of Jesus Christ. Creation and time are the stages upon which God brings unto Himself, for His own glory and pleasure, a group of people who will know and enjoy Him for all eternity.

As individuals, we can see providence played out in the circumstances of our birth and upbringing—in who our parents are and their background, in where we were born, in the spiritual condition of those around us, and in our exposure to the message of the gospel. It is clearly God's providence that brings us to an environment in which the Holy Spirit brings us individually to saving faith in Jesus Christ.

God's providence plays a role in our salvation and in the process of our sanctification. The Holy Spirit is the primary instrument working internally in this process, and God uses providence to bring about the external forces that cause us to grow and mature. God orders the stages in our lives to bring us to the right settings for us to grow spiritually by bringing us in contact with the right people and the right circumstances according to our needs. Providence also plays a role in our protection, as God keeps us from situations and temptations He knows would be harmful to our spiritual growth.

It is interesting that the word *providence* never appears in the Bible, yet it is one of the major doctrines presented in both the Old and New Testaments. One of the most exhaustive displays of providence in the Bible can be found in Genesis 37–50, where we read of how God ordered the life of Joseph. This passage demonstrates the wonderful message that God is involved in the lives of His people and that He has a purpose for everything that touches us.

As we study the Scriptures and learn of our awesome God, we begin to better understand that wonderful verse from the book of Romans: "We know that God causes everything to work together for the good of those who love God and are called according to his purpose for them" (8:28).

When we don't see God's providence in our lives, we miss out on the opportunity to see Him at work through circumstances. We need to recognize His providence and praise Him daily for it.

ACTION STEP:

Think about times in your life when you can clearly recognize God's providence. Make a point from now on to watch for events that represent God's providential care for you.

FOR FURTHER READING:

The Hand of God: Finding His Care in All Circumstances
Alistair Begg

4
God's Knowledge

Oh, what a wonderful God we have! How great are his riches and wisdom and knowledge! How impossible it is for us to understand his decisions and his methods! For who can know what the Lord is thinking? Who knows enough to be his counselor? And who could ever give him so much that he would have to pay it back? For everything comes from him; everything exists by his power and is intended for his glory. To him be glory evermore. Amen (Romans 11:33–36).

The invention of the microchip, in the opinion of many, has brought about some of the most compelling changes to human civilization since the invention of the printing press. Its inception ushered in the "information age." Unbelievable amounts of data are now more available to more people on the World Wide Web than would ever have been imagined possible just a few short years ago. The ability to gain information has never been greater.

As amazing as the amount of available information is, it is nothing in comparison with God's infinite knowledge. When we begin to understand what the Bible tells us about God's *omniscience*—the attribute of knowing everything—we realize that God's knowledge is beyond anything we can fathom.

It is not possible for us as finite creatures to fully understand any of God's characteristics. Even though God's omniscience is beyond our comprehension, we may draw great confidence in the wonderful truth of

God's all-encompassing knowledge. From the beginning to the end, God knows all. His knowledge is not limited by time. This is important because it tells us that nothing has ever caught God off guard or by surprise. From a position of knowing all, God continues to work out His plans, which were determined before the foundation of the world.

God knows every star by name, but, more importantly, He knows every human who was ever born or who is yet to be born. He knows the moment of our birth, and He knows the number of days that will make up our lives. God knows every hair on every head and every thought in every mind. God knows every cell that forms our parts. He knows our every heartbeat and every breath we draw.

God knows about every prayer ever prayed and every moment spent worshiping Him. God knows our every action and deed—past, present, and future—and He knows our motivations. Nothing has ever been hidden from God. It is wonderful to realize that God knows when our intentions are good and when we suffer for His name's sake.

We believers should continually reflect on this wonderful attribute of God in order that we might live better lives, being mindful that nothing is hidden from God.

ACTION STEP:

Look up and read the following Scriptures that tell us about God's omniscience: Psalm 139:1–18 and Isaiah

40:26–28. Think about what it means to you personally that God knows everything, even the things hidden from our sight.

FOR FURTHER READING:

God: Discover His Character
chapters 8 and 9, pp. 83–100
Bill Bright

5

Names and Titles of Jesus

Because of this, God raised him up to the heights of heaven and gave him a name that is above every other name, so that at the name of Jesus every knee will bow, in heaven and on earth and under the earth, and every tongue will confess that Jesus Christ is Lord, to the glory of God the Father (Philippians 2:9–11).

There are multitudes who know the name *Jesus* on a casual basis. Sadly, though, they never move beyond this surface knowledge, thus missing out on this life's greatest blessing—to truly and personally know the Lord of glory, Jesus Christ.

From Genesis to Revelation, the main theme of the Bible is the Person of God's Son, the second Person of the trinity. There are more than three hundred references in the Bible to the God-man, Jesus Christ. Let's take a look at just a few from the gospel of John and see what we can learn about the names and titles of Jesus.

In the eighth chapter of John, Jesus told the Pharisees, a group of religious leaders of His time, that He was the "I Am." This meant He was the eternal Son of God, existing before the beginning of time and continuing to exist forever beyond time, and that He created and sustained all things. He was telling the Pharisees that He was and is and will forever be God, the Lord Jesus Christ.

The first verse of the gospel of John states, "In the beginning was the Word, and the Word was with God, and the Word was God" (1:1 NKJV). The Bible tells us in Genesis 1:1 that God has always existed; in the *New Living Translation* of John 1:1 this is put, "In the beginning the Word already existed." When time and space began, He was there. "The Word was God" (NKJV) means that Jesus Christ was distinct in personality and that He was and is God, just as the Father and the Holy Spirit are God.

We also see in John 1 another of Jesus' titles: "the Lamb of God, which taketh away the sin of the world" (1:29 KJV). Jesus Christ came to earth to bear the sins of those who received Him. He bore the penalty for sin on the cross when He sacrificed His own life.

In what is the most recognized verse in the Bible, Christ is referred to as God's "only begotten Son" (John 3:16 KJV). We see here the immense love of God that caused Him to send His only Son to become human and die in our place.

As we come to chapter 4 of John's gospel, we see one of the more familiar titles of Jesus: Messiah (v. 25). There are references all through Scripture to the coming Messiah, God's provision for mankind's need. Jesus Christ was that Messiah, the Anointed One of God who would make salvation possible.

Another familiar title of Jesus in the gospel of John is "the bread of life." We read in the sixth chapter that Jesus addressed a large crowd and told them, "I am the bread of life: he that cometh to me shall never hunger; and he that believeth on me shall never thirst" (v. 35 KJV). Many of those who came to hear Jesus sought earthly bread, but He stressed that He came to give them eternal, life-giving bread.

In chapter 11, before raising Lazarus from the dead, He tells Lazarus's sister Martha, "I am the resurrection and the life" (11:25).

John 14:6 (KJV) summarizes who Jesus was and the purpose of His ministry: "Jesus saith unto them, 'I am the way, the truth, and the life.'" There are many false ways, but Jesus Christ is the only way to come to God. He is also the truth. In a world full of lies and deception, here is absolute truth. And He is life. Jesus Christ created and sustains life, and one day He will share His eternal life with those who belong to Him.

Be sure you know Jesus as the Bible reveals Him and that you are going to spend eternity with the One whose name is "above every name."

ACTION STEP:

Write out the "I am" verses from the gospel of John and memorize them. Think about what these verses say about who Jesus is and what that means to you as a believer.

FOR FURTHER READING:

The Names of Christ
T. C. Horton and Charles E. Hurlburt

6
Truth

His disciples came and asked him, "Why do you always tell stories when you talk to the people?" Then he explained to them, "You have been permitted to understand the secrets of the Kingdom of Heaven, but others have not. To those who are open to my teaching, more understanding will be given, and they will have an abundance of knowledge. But to those who are not listening, even what they have will be taken away from them. That is why I tell these stories, because people see what I do, but they don't really see. They hear what I say, but they don't really hear, and they don't understand (Matthew 13:10–13).

Believers in the Lord Jesus Christ enjoy countless benefits, not the least of which is the knowledge of truth. One of the foundations of our faith is that the Bible is the fountain of truth. The Bible is God's chosen instrument to provide us with the knowledge of who He is. The written Word demonstrates different facets of God's nature. It reveals a clear explanation of the world's digression to its current condition. Most importantly, it discloses what we can and need to do to change individually, as a family, as a community, and as a nation.

The Bible is the Holy Spirit's primary tool to lead and instruct believers in the way they should live. It is truly the library of life for a Christian, and it reveals the principles God has put into place to govern human lives and history.

One of these principles is found in the thirteenth

chapter of the gospel of Matthew, and it can be summarized like this: Provided truth must be acted upon to be retained. When truth is not embraced and applied, it will be lost.

This principle is evident in every area of life, especially in the spiritual life. God has so ordered His creation that if we do not respond to truth, we will suffer the consequences. As the Lord indicated in Matthew 13:12, those who are open to the truth will be given more, but those who do not listen will lose what little they have. The point is simple: We either learn and grow in our walk with Christ or we lose what we once had. This helps explain why so many believers are not growing in their faith in the Son of God and why we see more and more spiritual shallowness in the church body.

This principle sheds a great deal of light on what has been happening to the United States over the past fifty years. As a nation, we continue to neglect God's truth and, consequently, are losing the foundation upon which our nation was built. The light we once possessed, which was rooted in the absolutes of God's truth, has been lost. If you study history, you can see how this trend has played itself out in other nations, such as the United Kingdom.

An old hymn titled "Trust and Obey" captures this simple declaration. It is remarkably simple, yet astonishingly profound—trust and obey, for if we don't, we forfeit what we had once secured and, eventually, sacrifice the ability to trust God. Then, we lose our love for our Lord.

The Lord Jesus spoke of this condition to the church of Ephesus in the book of Revelation. "Look how far you have fallen from your first love! Turn back to me again and work as you did at first. If you don't, I will come and remove your lampstand from its place among the churches" (Revelation 2:5).

How great is our need to understand and apply this great principle of holding to the truth our Lord teaches in the written Word.

ACTION STEP:

Read Matthew 13:10–17 from the New International Version *or the* New Living Translation *and focus on the central message of these verses. Write a summary sentence that captures this profound principle of holding to truth.*

FOR FURTHER READING:

Two Cities, Two Loves: Christian Responsibility in a Crumbling Culture
chapter 7, pp. 139–57
James Montgomery Boice

7
Angels

Then I looked again, and I heard the singing of thousands and millions of angels around the throne and the living beings and the elders. And they sang in a mighty chorus: "The Lamb is worthy—the Lamb who was killed. He is worthy to receive power and riches and wisdom and strength and honor and blessing" (Revelation 5:11–12).

It has been said that the best way to spot a counterfeit is to be totally familiar with the real thing. This statement can be applied to many things, and it is certainly the case when we consider the subject of angels.

Over the past few years, the fascination and preoccupation with angels has mushroomed. Some gift stores now have entire sections dedicated to "angel stuff." Stories abound about encounters with angels and the roles they have played in people's lives. A recent movie portrayed an angel who came to minister to a preacher's wife. A current hit TV program features a new story every week about an encounter with an angel.

People today have had tremendous exposure to stories about angelic beings, so the question to ask is, Do these stories and accounts reveal to us any truth about angels?

In my opinion, the answer, sadly enough, would be no. Much of what is presented about angels today is focused on entertainment and is nothing more than fanciful tales. However, many believers are distracted by this type of foolishness and lose sight of the wonderful truth about God's holy angels. There is also the danger of mistaken identity. People can believe they have met a holy angel when in reality they have actually met a fallen angel. For this reason, we need to review what the Bible reveals about angels.

In the beginning, God created millions of angels and a representative human He called Adam. Each group reflected some of the characteristics of God. Both were made in God's image, so both had intellect, emotions, and will. Both were created to worship and serve God, but at different points in time, sin manifested itself in both angels and man. The Bible tells us that a great multitude of the angels chose to sin and rebel against God, who chose to save none of these fallen angels. Their fate for all eternity was sealed.

On the other hand, God made a way for fallen humankind to be brought back into fellowship with Himself. This truth of Scripture should reinforce the special grace and mercy God has shown to man by providing His only begotten Son to die in our place so that we could live eternally.

As children of God whose salvation is assured through Jesus Christ, we should note the example angels provide in their joy and obedience in worshiping their Creator. They are properly consumed in this exercise.

God created angels to accomplish specific purposes, one of which should be especially precious to all believers. The Bible tells us that angels keep watch over those whose names God has recorded in the Lamb's Book of Life. God sovereignly watches over each of us, and His holy angels play a role in that protection. We need to remember that God created all things and that all things are subject to His power and rule. God still limits what Satan, the chief fallen angel, and all his followers may do.

An understanding of angels helps remind believers that there are two worlds—the physical world we occupy now and the spirit world we will someday join. There is a very special appointment with angels that awaits each believer. At the moment of death, angels have the God-given privilege of transporting our born-again spirits to the throne of God and into the presence of the Lord Jesus Christ. There we will join with all those in heaven to His praise and for His glory.

ACTION STEP:

Angels appear frequently in the story of Christ's birth in Luke 1 and 2 and elsewhere in Luke in connection with Christ and with believers. Take time to look up Luke: 2:15; 4:10; 9:26; 12:8; 12:9; 15:10; 16:22; 20:36; and 24:23. Reflect on how these verses reinforce the role of angels in the believer's life.

FOR FURTHER READING:

Angels: Elect and Evil
C. Fred Dickason

Section 2

GOD FOR ALL

8

Knowing God's Plan

"My thoughts are completely different from yours," says the LORD*. "And my ways are far beyond anything you could imagine. For just as the heavens are higher than the earth, so are my ways higher than your ways and my thoughts higher than your thoughts. The rain and snow come down from the heavens and stay on the ground to water the earth. They cause the grain to grow, producing seed for the farmer and bread for the hungry. It is the same with my word. I send it out, and it always produces fruit. It will accomplish all I want it to, and it will prosper everywhere I send it" (Isaiah 55:8–11).*

The Bible makes clear that no one can know or understand the mind of God apart from what He has revealed to us in Scripture. Within His sovereignty, which is the biblical teaching that God controls and orders all things and is the supreme ruler of the entire universe, there are mysteries beyond our comprehension.

We often question much of what happens in life and struggle with things that don't appear to make sense, yet the Bible specifically tells us that God governs all the affairs of His creation. God has a plan for all things, and everything that happens contributes to the fulfillment of that plan. Knowing this truth, believers should trust God and look toward eternity, when we will grow in our understanding of God's purposes.

While we are limited in what we can know regarding God's plans, the Bible does reveal much of what is ahead. The Word tells us what will ultimately happen to our world, to the universe, and to every soul that has ever been born. The Bible charts the future of the Jewish people and the fate of the Jewish nation. But by far the most detailed plans revealed in Scripture are those the Lord has revealed for His children as believers in Jesus Christ.

Knowing this, we need to put reading and studying the Bible at the top of our priorities. I have discovered through my own experiences and those of others that the more we read and study God's Word, the more we recognize how it influences and guides and instructs us in every detail of life. When we read God's Word and allow the Holy Spirit to illuminate it to our hearts and minds, we learn what God desires for us.

The Holy Spirit, working inspirationally through various authors, has given us this supernatural library of instructions. The Bible provides us specific and personal instructions we can apply to our everyday lives. From this map, God's Word, we can find direction and answers to the questions confronting us.

Only God knows when we are walking according to His purposes, and He will use the Word to bring us in line with those plans. That is why we can read a particular Scripture verse thousands of times without special application to ourselves, but then, as the Holy Spirit illuminates our hearts and minds, we find that the verse suddenly takes on personal meaning and gives personal direction. This is primarily how God gives believers' lives direction.

A believer who is not actively and consistently reading and studying the Bible will not be equipped to live the life God intends. This is why so many Christians live far below the standards God desires for them, are weak in their faith, do not show forth the power of God, and have so little influence on the lost world.

If we want to know God's plan, we have to go to the Scriptures. When we do that, the enrichment of life we receive will transform us into productive and fulfilled children of God.

ACTION STEP:

Take some time to honestly answer these questions:

1. *How much time do I spend in daily Bible reading?*
2. *How often do I study a portion of Scripture?*
3. *Do I ever see God unfolding His plan for me through my reading of the Word? In what ways?*

FOR FURTHER READING:

Discovering God's Will
Sinclair B. Ferguson

9

God's Wrath

For the wrath of God is revealed from heaven against all ungodliness and unrighteousness of men, who suppress the truth in unrighteousness (Romans 1:18 NASB).

I recently saw a movie that conveyed in a realistic and moving way a message about war. This movie was a look at the greatest military conflict our world has yet seen—World War II. It gave the viewer a real sense of the horrors of war and accurately portrayed the carnage of the D day landing on the beaches of Normandy. It gave the audience an authentic picture of the men who made up the Allied forces and their conflict with the Axis powers.

Sadly, memories of World War II are fading away as the older generation passes from the scene. That history is lost to most of the younger generation today. So the movie I saw was a needed reminder to the new generation of the awful cost of war and the heavy price so many paid for our freedom.

We believers need another kind of reminder today. We need to remember that a war far greater than any fought on any physical battlefield rages at this very moment. It is the battle God wages against Satan and sin. Although many people do not realize it, this war is being fought in the life of every human being on the planet. Like World War II, this war involves areas of intense conflict. We can see the casualties of this great spiritual battle everywhere in the form of ruined lives and lost souls. And we will see the casualties of this war in the judgment to come.

God still judges sin. The Bible tells us that His wrath is poured out against all unrighteousness, that those whose sins are not forgiven through Christ face the coming wrath at the Great White Throne judgment.

God's judgment is also demonstrated when He removes His restraining presence and allows a nation to pursue its own course. I believe this is precisely what is happening to America. For example, over the past forty years we have slowly moved from an acceptance of the sexual revolution of the sixties to the sanctioning and approval of homosexuality.

We are now witnessing the impact of evil minds in our society. As Romans 1:29 said would happen, our culture is full of every kind of wickedness, greed, hatred, envy, murder, fighting, deception, malicious behavior, and gossip. No one can honestly argue that our overall society is not in a sad and tragic condition. And without a renewed presence of God, the trend toward evil in our nation will only worsen.

As horrible as God's current wrath is, there is still hope for us in the person of the Lord Jesus Christ. The Bible makes clear, however, that God is storing up His ultimate wrath, which will be delivered at the end of time. This will be His eternal wrath of hell for all who have not been covered by the blood of the Lamb of God.

When we approach the subject of God's wrath, we need to understand it within the setting of His holiness contrasted against sin. Pastor John MacArthur, the noted Bible expositor, put it this way in his commentary *Romans 1–8:* "God's attributes are balanced in divine perfection. If He had no righteous anger and wrath, He would not be God, just as surely as He would not be God without His gracious love."

Believers need to recognize and understand the subject of God's wrath and need to explain to the lost the consequences of sin as it is revealed in Romans 1:18–32.

ACTION STEP:

Read Romans 1:18–32, then think about how this passage relates to what is happening in our culture today. Prayerfully consider how you can do spiritual battle against the forces of sin and death.

FOR FURTHER READING:

Romans 1–8, The MacArthur New Testament Commentary series
pp. 59–68
John MacArthur, Jr.

10
God's Love

For God so loved the world that He gave His only begotten Son, that whoever believes in Him should not perish but have everlasting life (John 3:16 NKJV).

It is a mistake to engage in any thoughts of God without using the Bible as the reference point. The Bible is God's chosen vehicle to reveal all truth that is necessary for us to know of Him. This is especially true when we address the subject of God's love.

Love in our day is defined in terms of the human understanding of the word. This kind of "love" is superficial, emotion-driven, and prone to failure because of wrong motivations. This is clearly not what the Bible reveals to us about God's love.

The Bible tells us in 1 John 4:8 that "God is love." As He is in all of His attributes, God is perfect in His love. Going a step further, love is His very nature. His love is uninfluenced by any need or response on our part. This is shown most clearly in the fact that there was nothing about us that caused God to love us. In our sin, we were totally unlovable, and yet Christ died for us. This is what God's love is all about, what John 3:16 is all about.

It could be said that John 3:16, probably one of the best-known of all Bible verses and without a doubt one of the most important, summarizes the main message of the Bible. Martin Luther referred to it as the "minigospel." For millions of people, John 3:16 was the first verse they memorized. For countless others, it represents the greatest message they will ever hear.

John 3:16 declares a truth believers should never stop being thankful for and a message believers should never tire of proclaiming. An understanding of this one verse helps us to understand why people go so far as to buy tickets to professional sporting events in order to display large signs and banners with John 3:16 spelled out.

John 3:16 states simply a message we all need to hear, and that message is God's love. Tragically, though, much of the world gives little notice to this message, and many go so far as to question the existence of God's love. Sadly, even many professing Christians have an inaccurate and distorted understanding of what God's love really is and how it corresponds to His other attributes.

The gospel of John focuses mainly on Jesus' life and teachings and helps explain the theological implication of this narrative. The core message of John is summarized in chapter 3, verse 16. God knew sin would enter into the world, so before the beginning of creation the Holy Trinity established a plan to address the sin problem.

God's love for the world is demonstrated in the fact that He knew it would be necessary to sacrifice the second Person of the Trinity, yet He sent Him anyway. God clearly anticipated the need of the Cross, yet He loved us enough to send His Son. He loved us before the foundation of the world, knowing we would be slaves to sin and unrighteousness and be His enemies. Yet He sacrificially gave His Son, who would be lifted up on the cross, so that whoever believed in Him would not be forever separated from God's love and light, but would live forever in a state of indescribable bliss in God's presence.

God has provided the sacrifice, and it is available to whoever believes. Christ died for us and for our sins. Because He was totally man and totally God, He was able to bridge the gap between sinful man and the Holy God.

ACTION STEP:

Write out John 3:16 on an index card and underline the ten main words. Think about the significance and the message of these words. Personalize this verse and realize that God loved you so much that He gave His Son.

FOR FURTHER READING:

For God So Loved
chapter 3, pp. 30–99
J. Sidlow Baxter

11
The Atonement

But He was wounded for our transgressions, He was bruised for our iniquities; the chastisement for our peace was upon Him, and by His stripes we are healed. All we like sheep have gone astray; we have turned, every one, to his own way; and the LORD has laid on Him the iniquity of us all (Isaiah 53:5–6 NKJV).

As we usher in the new millennium, it is interesting to read about and watch various summaries and analyses of the twentieth century. By all accounts, it was an amazing period of time marked by events, inventions, and discoveries that influenced most of the world's population and changed the way humans live.

Many major occurrences have altered the course of history throughout the centuries, but one episode outweighs all others in its significance, and that is the crucifixion of the second Person of the Trinity, Jesus Christ. For the majority of the world, history is divided into two segments: the time before Jesus' birth (B.C.) and the time after His birth (A.D., *anno Domini*, Latin for "in the year of our Lord"). All believers from the time of Adam looked forward to Christ's arrival, and all who have since been born again look back at it.

When we understand what actually took place at the Crucifixion, we understand why it was truly the most important event in history. The Bible reveals the importance of the Crucifixion and what it means for all who have and will come to a saving faith in the Lord Jesus Christ.

On the cross, Christ accomplished what we call the Atonement, which is the work of paying the price for our sins so that we could receive salvation. This act demonstrated the love of God in providing a way of salvation, and it shows the righteousness of God in that He required payment be made for our sins.

God sent Christ to be an acceptable sacrifice for our sins. Because Jesus Christ is God and is eternal, He could accept the eternal punishment, which was God's demand for sin. Jesus Christ was also a perfect sacrifice because He lived a perfectly sinless life. God poured out on His Son the wrath for sins from the time of Adam until the end of this world. The Bible makes clear that Jesus satisfied the holy requirement for the payment of our sin debt and that the Atonement was completed and secured for eternity.

Jesus Christ's finished work on the cross allows all who will believe in Him to be reconciled with God the Father. All of humanity was separated from God at the Fall, and only through Christ can we have reconciliation. As believers, we have been redeemed from the bondage to Satan and sin and no longer need to fear God's eternal wrath for sin.

We should rejoice when we think of the awesome sacrifice our Savior made for us. Our hearts should be flooded with thanksgiving for the love our heavenly Father poured out on us when He gave His only begotten Son. We need to live daily in the shadow of the cross of Calvary and in the atoning work of our Lord Jesus Christ.

ACTION STEP:

Locate and read the Crucifixion account in the Synoptic Gospels (Matthew, Mark, and Luke), and meditate on the account of our Savior's sacrifice for us—for you. Take time to thank God for making a way for you to be saved from His eternal wrath.

FOR FURTHER READING:

The Atonement: Its Meaning and Significance
Leon Morris

12
Salvation

God saved you by his special favor when you believed. And you can't take credit for this; it is a gift from God. Salvation is not a reward for the good things we have done, so none of us can boast about it (Ephesians 2:8–9).

There are many interpretations and definitions of the word *salvation.* I believe that a lack of understanding of what the Bible says about this subject is one reason so many professing Christians do not have true saving faith.

By his very nature, man tends to elevate himself while at the same time reducing God to a deity of his own liking. That affects the way we approach the subject of salvation. We tend to be self-centered instead of God-centered in our approach to salvation.

Salvation is of *God* from beginning to end. The Bible tells us that before the foundation of the world, God chose those whose names would be written in the Lamb's Book of Life. God orders every circumstance in the lives of those He has chosen so that they will be drawn to Him. Then, at some point in the earthly life of the called person, God performs the first step in the process of salvation, which is called regeneration. This is an act of the Holy Spirit, totally independent of man's actions, that begins new spiritual life in the heart of a lost, spiritually dead sinner. At the point of regeneration, God enacts a covenant with the newly saved person that testifies that this enlivened person is justified by the sacrifice of Jesus Christ on the cross. Justification is a divine act whereby an infinitely holy

God declares a believing sinner to be righteous and acceptable before Him because Christ has borne the sinner's transgressions.

Up to this point in his or her salvation, the newly saved person has played no role whatsoever in the process—it is all of God, who has determined and executed the salvation. It is an undeserved, unmerited, and uninfluenced gift from almighty God. God's primary purpose for this act is to demonstrate His wondrous character and to bring Himself glory forever.

The next step in the salvation process is that of God's giving the gifts of repentance and faith to the newly redeemed sinner. It is at this juncture that the believer becomes aware of the glorious and mysterious act God has performed.

During the process of salvation, the newly saved person begins to understand and walk in God's love, which then begins to work its way into the new creation. It is also at this time that the Holy Spirit comes to live within the heart of the believer, providing guidance, leading, and conviction of sin. This process is called *sanctification,* and it serves to give the new believer assurance that he or she has truly been born again.

Regeneration and *justification* are onetime acts of God in the life of a believer, but in another sense, *salvation* is a lifelong process in which the believer goes through times of victory and times of defeat, times of joy and times of sadness, and times of growth and times of failure. As God works in the life of His child, this new creation becomes more and more recognizable as one of God's children. One of the great delights of being a believer is to see the work of grace God has done in the life of one who has walked with the Lord for many years. It is a little taste of heaven for any believer, and it can be a great encouragement to the new convert.

One day, at the end of this life, every believer will receive final salvation when he or she is glorified. This is the time when we will enter into our final home in the presence of our heavenly Father. This is the salvation of the whole person.

It is a great tragedy that so many have been led astray by a false gospel that does not correctly reflect the truths about salvation from the Word of God. It is vital that we know these truths and share them with those around us.

Ultimately, the most important question a living soul can ask is this: Have I been truly saved? Be certain you can say yes to this question.

ACTION STEP:

*Secure a Bible dictionary (*The New Unger's Bible Dictionary *is a good one) and look up the following terms:* salvation, regeneration, justification, atonement, sanctification, *and* glorification. *Then write their definitions on three-by-five index cards. Take time to read over and reflect on these definitions.*

FOR FURTHER READING:

The Heart of Christianity: What It Means to Believe in Jesus
chapter 9, pp. 103–13
Ron Rhodes

13
Hope

Without wavering, let us hold tightly to the hope we say we have, for God can be trusted to keep his promise (Hebrews 10:23).

Recently, while I was out, my wife received a phone call from the son of a longtime friend. When I returned home, she gave me the sad news that our friend had died after a long battle with cancer.

Death is never pleasant, and sorrow accompanies the sober reality of a soul's departure into eternity. Yet for my friend, who was a believer, I rest in the fact that he is now with the Lord in glory.

I am happy that I visited him just a week before he died and enjoyed a sweet time of fellowship with him. During those moments, I was struck by something that has caused me to ponder the subject of hope. I found it very moving that my dear friend, so near death, still held onto hope. Deep within him was an expectation that he could be healed by a special intervention of the Lord Jesus.

I did not challenge his hope, for I too believed it was possible, even though it did not seem likely. At that time, though, we both held to the sure hope of the Resurrection and to Christ's promise that to be absent from the body was to be in the presence of the Lord. As believers, this hope is always with us, so we rest in the assurance of this wonderful truth.

In contrast, a few weeks before my friend died, an awful event took place in Atlanta, Georgia. A deranged gunman killed twelve people and then took his own life. A short time later, authorities found a note the killer had left. In it, he made a statement that jumped out at me. He said that he had lost all hope and did not anticipate that he would live very long. This killer had come to a point where he could see no hope and so concluded that he no longer had a reason to live.

This type of despair is far more common than we would care to think, especially among our young people. Suicide among teens is one of the major causes of death in that age group. This despair has also spurred an increase in senseless acts of violence that precede young people taking their own lives.

When someone reaches the point of no hope, Satan has won a great victory in that person's life, and tragedy can follow. Then only the love of Christ can offer hope.

But there is a kind of hope that could be properly labeled a "false hope." Many people have a form of religion and faith they have created for themselves. It usually involves taking selected thoughts and ideas—some "truths" from one religion and some from another—and modifying them to reflect current thinking and trends. From this comes a belief system that conforms to the particular individual's comfort zone. This kind of hope is strongly influenced by the concepts and views of this world, not from the Bible. Sadly, there are millions who are comfortably resting in this condition but who are one second away from entering an eternity without hope.

Even as I am writing, that thought challenges me to become even more dedicated to proclaiming the truth that real hope can be found. As I indicated in the story of my brother in Christ, it is only in Christ that there is any true hope, and it is only those who are in Christ who will live eternally in the presence of the Lord in heaven. Be sure that yours is the absolute hope that is based on Christ alone.

ACTION STEP:

Think about where you have placed your hope, then look up these hope-related verses in the Bible and ask yourself if your hope is based on these Scriptures:

Psalms 33:18; 65:5; 146:5
Proverbs 10:28
Lamentations 3:22–24
Colossians 1:4–6
Hebrews 6:17–18

FOR FURTHER READING:

Hope: The Heart's Great Quest
chapter 8, pp. 113–29
David Ackman

Section 3

GOD WITH US

14
Faith and Repentance

When the people heard this, they were cut to the heart and said to Peter and the other apostles, "Brothers, what shall we do?" Peter replied, "Repent and be baptized, every one of you, in the name of Jesus Christ for the forgiveness of your sins" (Acts 2:37–38 NIV).

Billy Graham is one of the best-known and, by many standards, most-respected figures in the world. For decades, he has held a prominent platform from which he has preached the Good News of the gospel to millions.

Recently, while appearing on the national television program *Larry King Live*, Billy was asked if he still needs to repent of sins. "Absolutely!" he answered. "Every day!" He went on to say that the longer he lives the more aware of his own sinfulness he becomes. He made clear that believers never stop repenting, because we all continue to sin.

When Reverend Graham delivers the gospel message, he always starts by talking about the need for repentance. He tells his listeners that they need to recognize themselves as sinners who have violated God's laws and are helpless within themselves to change that fact. He tells them that they need a change of mind toward God and a change of attitude toward God's judgment of sin. He reminds his listeners that God has decreed that the wages of sin is death and that at the end of the world all sin not covered by the atoning sacrifice of Christ's blood will demand eternal punishment. He then calls his audience to accept through faith and repentance God's offer of salvation.

True repentance is best understood first as a change of mind and attitude toward who Jesus Christ is and who you are as a lost sinner. True repentance leads to a change in behavior that is the result of a change of mind and heart. It establishes a new life that is lived by faith in Jesus Christ and directed by the Word of God, the Bible. In short, repentance means you turn from your way and go God's way.

Faith and repentance are two components that constitute what the Bible calls *saving faith*. We cannot be "born again" without both true repentance and faith in the person and work of Jesus Christ.

It is also important to understand where the ability to repent and have faith in Christ comes from. The Bible says both are supernatural gifts from God that represent an outward expression of an inward work the Holy Spirit does in the heart. This is what we call *regeneration.*

No one can have true repentance and saving faith until God has given him a new heart. True Christianity is not something that starts on the outside and works its way in. It is just the opposite. It starts with God's making alive what was spiritually dead. It is from this point that everything else flows. It is from a new heart that our spiritual eyes are opened to the message of the gospel. It is through repentance and faith that we believe in Christ.

Examine yourself and be certain that God has done the work on your heart that produces faith, repentance, and a transformed life.

ACTION STEP:

Look up in a concordance the verses that contain the words faith *and* repentance. *Look up these verses in the Bible and then write a brief summary of each.*

FOR FURTHER READING:

The Way of Life: A Guide to Christian Belief and Experience
chapter 7, pp. 153–70
Charles Hodge

15
Justification

By Him everyone who believes is justified from all things from which you could not be justified by the law of Moses (Acts 13:39 NKJV).

On a recent edition of an evening current events television program, I witnessed the court proceeding of a man who had served twelve years on death row for the murder of a nurse. After years of trying to get his case reopened based on the new technology of DNA testing, it was conclusively proven that this individual was innocent. I watched as the judge told the prisoner, who had been brought to the court under armed guard, "You are now a free man and can leave this court immediately." At that moment, this person went from being under the judgment of the court to being free.

It was moving to watch this take place, but it reminded me that there is a far greater drama continually playing itself out. In this drama truly guilty people are being declared free and allowed to begin living a new life that will someday lead to an eternity with God in heaven.

In the court of heaven, the final Judge of all, God Himself, pronounces guilty sinners like us—those under the curse of eternal damnation—free from the sentence of eternal death and free from a life of slavery to sin. This declaration is made possible because of the imputed (to lay the credit, responsibility, or blame for something upon someone else) righteousness of Christ, which is based on His sinless life and His atoning sacrifice at Calvary. It is the great exchange that must occur in order for lost sinners to be made righteous in Christ and to become reconciled to God. This is the message and the heart of the Christian faith.

That is what the Bible means when it says, "Being justified freely by His grace through the redemption that is in Christ Jesus" (Romans 3:24 NKJV). This foundational truth of the Christian faith is called the *doctrine of justification.* It is the God-given truth that states that when someone comprehends and accepts by faith the message of the gospel, he is justified before God. The reality of that acceptance demonstrates that God the Holy Spirit has regenerated that individual and has set in motion a wonderful plan for a life in Christ.

At the core of this doctrine is the fact that the triune God pardons and accepts sinners who by faith believe that He displayed His wrath by condemning and punishing sin through the death of Jesus Christ at the cross of Calvary. The just demands of a holy God required a perfect sacrifice, and God displayed His unfathomable love in that He was willing to accept Christ's death as a substitute in the place of sinners. Christ provided His perfect righteousness for the sinner. Only those who have that perfect righteousness will ever see heaven.

Justification is a transaction that is part of the process of salvation. It reinforces the fact that salvation is a free gift from God and that the saved sinner contributes nothing. It is all of grace. It is God's answer to the question, How can a man or woman become right with God?

ACTION STEP:

Take the time to think about what occurred when you were justified. Look up the word justified *in the Bible; then write down a simple outline of this doctrine.*

FOR FURTHER READING:

Faith Alone
chapter 4, pp. 67–91
R. C. Sproul

16
Adoption

For as many as are led by the Spirit of God, these are sons of God. For you did not receive the spirit of bondage again to fear, but you received the Spirit of adoption by whom we cry out, "Abba, Father." The Spirit Himself bears witness with our spirit that we are children of God, and if children, then heirs—heirs of God and joint heirs with Christ, if indeed we suffer with Him, that we may also be glorified together (Romans 8:14–17 NKJV).

Of all the blessings Adam and Eve enjoyed in the garden before the Fall, I believe none was more special than the intimate fellowship they had with the triune God. In a sense, I am sure that they felt as children feel in the security and shelter of home with their parents. In God's presence the first man and woman knew only peace, comfort, and joy. They had sweet fellowship with their Creator, Lord, and heavenly Father.

Tragically, though, Adam and Eve lost this wonderfully personal and open relationship because of their sin of disobedience. The Bible tells us that sin entered the world through one man, Adam, and that since then the world has never been as it was intended to be. Daily we witness the consequences of sin on the human race. The Fall affects every element of our lives, most notably our relationship with God.

That intimate relationship we were meant to enjoy with God can be restored only when we accept by faith the Good News of the gospel of Jesus Christ and repent of our sins. This restored relationship is called *adoption* in the Bible, and it is another element of the wondrous miracle of salvation.

This adoption is not part of *regeneration* (when a spiritually dead sinner is made alive by the power of God), nor is it *justification* (God's declaration that affirms a sinner is made righteous by the finished work of Christ on the cross). *Adoption* is when God makes us part of His family. It is then that we become children of God, brothers and sisters to Christ, and joint heirs with Jesus. At that time, we receive the awesome privilege of calling the Creator God "*Abba*, Father" and of having access to Him at any time. As our heavenly Father, God is concerned for our well-being and knows perfectly what all our needs are even before we ask or recognize them.

As believers, we have this special relationship with almighty God. Yet many have little understanding of this privilege, or at least it does not play a major role in their daily lives. Many believers do not enjoy the intimacy and closeness with God that He so longs to have with all of His children.

One of the best ways we can grow in our intimacy with God is to become more conscious of that very special gift our heavenly Father has given us—the gift of the Holy Spirit. The more sensitive we become to the leading of the Holy Spirit, the stronger our love and devotion toward our heavenly Father will grow. As we grow in our love for and devotion to the Father, we will become more aware of our own sinfulness and of the need to rely on the work of the Holy Spirit. The

Bible makes clear that we are called to imitate our Father and to become holy as He is holy.

As we continue to learn more about the attributes and the character of God, our relationship with Him becomes more precious to us. The Bible tells us that as we progress in living a life that is pleasing to Him, we actually bring glory and honor to Him.

ACTION STEP:

Answer the following question: What is your daily relationship to your heavenly Father? Read about some of the earlier saints who had intimacy with God and think about ways in which you can draw closer to Him every day.

FOR FURTHER READING:

Knowing God
chapter 19, pp. 200–229
J. I. Packer

17
Sanctification

I am crucified with Christ: nevertheless I live; yet not I, but Christ liveth in me: and the life which I now live in the flesh I live by the faith of the Son of God, who loved me, and gave himself for me (Galatians 2:20 KJV*).*

The world is full of self-help books, programs, and seminars aimed at helping people make changes in their lives. No doubt some of them are of some benefit. But when weighed against the absolute truth of the Word of God and its power to help us make permanent transformations, we can see that they provide only partial answers at best.

As believers and disciples of Jesus Christ, we know that real change comes when we receive a new heart, and that is a gift from God to all who by faith receive the Good News of the gospel. When we first put our faith in Christ for our salvation, it is a onetime change that in many ways is just the beginning of a life of faith. It is at this point that sanctification comes into play.

Sanctification is the process that God, by the power of the Holy Spirit, uses to take a new believer and advance that person from a state of vulnerability to sin to a state of holiness. This process involves a decision on the believer's part to draw upon the wisdom and strength available from the Holy Spirit so that the person can make real and lasting changes in how he or she lives.

Misunderstanding and misapplication of this pivotal doctrine is a major reason for the lack of impact many believers have on the lost world around them.

When we examine some of the key points regarding the doctrine of sanctification, we can see how important this process is to the fulfilling of God's plans for our lives.

The first thing we need to understand about sanctification is that our great need for change is part of God's plan. All of us, even those who appeared outwardly to be very good people, were enemies of God and lovers of self before we received salvation through Christ. It is only after we have been saved that we begin to move toward holiness and conformity to the likeness of Jesus Christ. Only the power of the Holy Spirit makes true and lasting change possible. This is why only true believers can be truly changed. Those who are not born again can make short-term changes and improvements, but they will never be truly transformed people.

One of the initial steps toward sanctification is to ask God to show you specific things you need to change. Many new converts immediately receive victory over sinful habits and evil desires. They may see instant transformation in some areas of their walk with the Lord. However, they may also find that change does not come as easily in other areas of their lives, and they may find themselves in a battle that takes time to win. Some sinful habits and choices actually become part of a person's personality, and it may take hard work, continued prayer, and endurance in order to see transformation in that area.

Even with that, there may be times when the new convert falls short. In that case, it is absolutely essential that the person recognize that it is Christ's power living within him or her that guarantees ultimate victory. We receive that power as we learn of Him and draw on Him and as we recognize our dependence on the Holy Spirit.

We all need to allow the Holy Spirit to rule in our lives. We also need to continually act on the truth of the Word of God. We need to be obedient to what is presented in the Scriptures, especially the Epistles, pertaining to our growth as believers.

Finally, we need to be involved in biblical friendships. We need to draw on the encouragement, guidance, and prayers of those with whom God has brought us into contact. We need to establish accountability with these people. Our relationships within the body of believers play a critical role in our sanctification.

ACTION STEP:

Can you think of some areas of your spiritual life where you have seen progress? How about areas where you need more change? Write both down, then thank God for the areas where you have been transformed and ask Him what steps you should take to make change in those other areas.

FOR FURTHER READING:

I Really Want to Change . . . So, Help Me God
chapter 1, pp. 25–41
James MacDonald

18
Glorification

It is the same way for the resurrection of the dead. Our earthly bodies, which die and decay, will be different when they are resurrected, for they will never die. Our bodies now disappoint us, but when they are raised, they will be full of glory. They are weak now, but when they are raised, they will be full of power. They are natural human bodies now, but when they are raised, they will be spiritual bodies. For just as there are natural bodies, so also there are spiritual bodies (1 Corinthians 15:42–44).

Glorification is the final step in God's wonderful plan of redemption. This step will take place at the second coming of the Lord Jesus, when He gives all believers—those who will be raised from the grave at His coming, as well as those still physically alive—a body like the one He received at His resurrection. At this time, Christ's work of redemption for all believers will be finished. The last effect of the Fall, physical death, will be erased for all those who have died in Christ or who are redeemed at His second coming.

God has provided analogies in nature that can help us better understand the process of glorification. In 1 Corinthians, the apostle Paul likens the body of a believer to a seed. He tells us that a believer's body is sown in a corruptible form. Even after our regeneration, or new birth, we retain a corruptible body that is subject to injury, disease, and, ultimately, death. Paul tells us that this body is sown in dishonor, fulfilling part of the original curse God announced after the Fall. It is sown in a weakness that is demonstrated in our failure to live as we should, in our propensity to sin even though we have received the power of the Holy Spirit.

Our bodies are natural and earthly. They were made from this earth and they will return to the earth. But God has promised that those who are in Christ will be raised from the dead in glorified bodies that will never again be subject to sin, disease, injury, or death. Our new bodies will be raised incorruptible and glorious. They will display the final victory over the curse of death. Our new bodies will be raised in power. Death could not contain our crucified Savior, and the same power that raised Him from the grave will bring forth all who are His own.

Finally, our new bodies will be forever free from sin. They will be the bodies God intended them to be from the beginning. They will be like Christ's own body in that they can be touched and seen and can receive food and drink. But they will be prepared to exist forever in the presence of the triune God.

All believers—those who are now with Christ in paradise and those who are still living—are awaiting the final step in our redemption. It is no wonder that from the time shortly after Christ's ascension to heaven until now, the church has been eagerly awaiting the second coming of the risen Lord. All believers should long for this great day and for the final gift of conversion, their glorified bodies.

> Behold, I tell you a mystery: We shall not all sleep, but we shall all be changed—in a moment, in the twinkling

of an eye, at the last trumpet. For the trumpet will sound, and the dead will be raised incorruptible, and we shall be changed. (1 Corinthians 15:51–52 NKJV)

Oh, for that last trumpet!

ACTION STEP:

Take time to read and study the last two chapters of 1 Corinthians. Try to imagine the difference between the body you have now and the glorified body you are promised in God's Word.

FOR FURTHER READING:

The Last Things
chapter 4, pp. 83–107
Paul Helm

19
Assurance

My sheep recognize my voice; I know them, and they follow me. I give them eternal life, and they will never perish. No one will snatch them away from me, for my Father has given them to me, and he is more powerful than anyone else (John 10:27–29).

A clear and correct understanding of the meaning of being *born again* will be decisive in the way a true believer lives. Nowhere is this more apparent than in the area of assurance. The idea of assurance is derived from the doctrine of eternal security. A common reference to this doctrine is "once saved, always saved."

Throughout most of church history, this issue has been a subject of strong disagreement. The great dividing line in this issue is the answer to the question, What role does the natural man play in the process of being born again? As always, we should go to the Word of God for the answers.

The place to start is to see what God has revealed to us about who He is. The Bible tells us God is above time and knows everything from beginning to end. Nothing catches God by surprise. Long before He formed the world, He knew everything that would ever happen (see chapter 4, "God's Knowledge"). In Romans 8:28–30 (NKJV), God gives us a glimpse of the process of salvation. This passage says He *foreknew* those He would love and *predestined*, or chose ahead of time, to *call* those people by the power of the Holy Spirit. It also says He will *justify* (see chapter 15,

"Justification") those He called. Finally, we read that those He foreknew, predestined, called, and justified will be *glorified.*

It is important to note that God is the One who carries out these steps. The Bible tells us that from start to finish, the new birth is a gift from God and that He is the "author and finisher of our faith" (Hebrews 12:2 NKJV).

Almighty God, the One who spoke the universe into being, the One who upholds all things, and the One who raises up and puts down mighty nations is able to carry out His purposes for those He loved before the foundation of the world. As we learn more of the attributes of God, we should rest more fully in God's plan of salvation. The wonderful truth of the Scriptures is that true believers can rest in the Father's plan, in the finished work of our Savior and Lord, and in the supernatural work of the Holy Spirit.

At the same time, though, this biblical doctrine can be applied incorrectly, which can provide an erroneous sense of assurance to those who are not truly regenerated. The Bible is clear that many will come before Jesus Christ thinking they have had a relationship with Him, but He will say, "Depart from Me, you who practice lawlessness!" (Matthew 7:22–23 NKJV).

Many people maintain the label "Christian" as an insurance policy they believe will provide them a ticket to heaven. The Evil One has deceived many with this false sense of security, and their "assurance" is more presumption than anything else. I am convinced that "false assurance" is one of Satan's greatest weapons against the church today. Countless numbers look at some past event when they made a decision for Christ —walking an aisle, asking Jesus into their hearts, or getting baptized—but in the subsequent years, the evidence of the transforming power of grace has not been manifested in their lives. Somehow, they presume that God doesn't mean what He says in His written Word. I can assure them that the Bible tells us that they are deceived and are still under the wrath of God.

Make sure your election and calling are sure. Examine your life and see how it measures up against the commandments of the Lord Jesus presented in the Bible.

ACTION STEP:

Take the time to answer these questions:

1. *Do I need to be perfect to reach heaven?*
2. *On what is my assurance of heaven based?*
3. *Does the Holy Spirit confirm my assurance of salvation?*
4. *What does the life of a truly saved person look like?*
5. *How does my life measure up?*

FOR FURTHER READING:

How You Can Be Sure That You Will Spend Eternity with God
chapters 5 and 6, pp. 89–124
Erwin W. Lutzer

Section 4

A GODLY LIFE

20
Loving God

"For I was hungry, and you fed me. I was thirsty, and you gave me a drink. I was a stranger, and you invited me into your home. I was naked, and you gave me clothing. I was sick, and you cared for me. I was in prison, and you visited me." Then these righteous ones will reply, "Lord, when did we ever see you hungry and feed you? Or thirsty and give you something to drink? Or a stranger and show you hospitality? Or naked and give you clothing? When did we ever see you sick or in prison, and visit you?" And the King will tell them, "I assure you, when you did it to one of the least of these my brothers and sisters, you were doing it to me!" (Matthew 25:35–40).

Since that early morning hour in mid-October 1980 when I cried out to God and found hope, peace, and forgiveness, I have never gotten over the love of God that was poured out in my soul that day. For the first time in my life, I began to realize what it means to truly love God. Over the many years since then, that love has grown ever stronger. I pray that it continues to deepen as more time passes, and I pray that others would come to know the love for God that fills my being.

Before that morning, I thought I loved God, but I discovered that the love I had was really for myself. True love for God is a supernatural gift that is a result of the transformation of the new birth. Sadly, there are vast numbers of professing Christians who outwardly express love for God but, as was my case, whose motivation for loving Him is to see what He can do for them, not what they can do for Him. I can tell you from personal experience and from what I have seen in the Word of God that once you truly experience His wondrous love, you will desire to love Him in return.

Over the past eighteen years, I have been richly blessed by reading and studying literally thousands of books on what it is to be a true believer in the Lord Jesus Christ and to truly love God. A wonderful book I read early in my Christian walk, and have since reread a number of times, is *Loving God* by Charles Colson. In chapter 22 the writer tells the moving story of a grandmother named Myrtie Howell, whose life was a classic example of the working of God's love in the heart of a believer, manifesting itself in the outpouring of kindness, service, and love to others. It also marks the distinction between those who truly possess God and those who do not. The story is an emotional one that captures the true essence of what loving God means.

Chuck Colson concludes the story by writing about his visit to a run-down "old folks' home" in Columbus, Georgia. Colson describes the building as a forlorn place of sadness, boredom, loneliness, and hopelessness. He contrasts that picture with his personal encounter with Grandma Howell. Like the others around her, she had known hardship and tragedy. The difference between her and the others was that she had come to understand the vanity and bleakness of life without God. By the power of the Holy Spirit, she had come to know the victory of selflessness and had been guided to her new calling of writing prisoners. Through her obedience in this ministry, she had come to enjoy the special blessing that comes from a dedication to serving God and others.

Chuck Colson concludes his story of Myrtie Howell with this burning statement: "And God gave me the final link in my search to learn what loving God really means: Myrtie Howell. To believe, to repent, to obey, to be holy, to bind up the brokenhearted, and to serve. Myrtie Howell knew all about loving God."

Ask God to open your eyes to what it really means to love Him. Look around you at all those in need and determine by God's grace that you will put action into the words *loving God.*

ACTION STEP:

Take some time to reflect on your attitude toward God. Ask yourself this key question: What am I doing that demonstrates that I truly love God, and is there something God is leading me to do?

FOR FURTHER READING:

Loving God
chapter 22, pp. 209–16
Chuck Colson

21

Fellowship

Then make me truly happy by agreeing wholeheartedly with each other, loving one another, and working together with one heart and purpose. Don't be selfish; don't live to make a good impression on others. Be humble, thinking of others as better than yourself. Don't think only about your own affairs, but be interested in others, too, and what they are doing (Philippians 2:2–4).

For many years I worked in the medical-health industry. During that time, I learned some basic facts about the makeup and function of the human body. The more I learned, the more conscious I became of just how "fearfully and wonderfully" we are made. The marvels of the body are in some ways like the marvels God created in the cosmos—many of the elements are beyond our comprehension. Yet with modern medicine, we have discovered much about how the body functions.

One thing I learned on this subject is that all parts of the anatomy are separate yet interrelated and interdependent. The apostle Paul used the analogy of the human body to help believers understand how the body of Christ, the church, needs to conduct itself. Though the church is made up of individuals, we are still interrelated and interdependent on one another.

The Bible is specific about just how critical we are "one to another." Romans 12:5 brings out the fact that we are all part of Christ's body and that we belong to and need each other. It also stresses that God has given each believer a specific role to work within that sphere and that He has equipped each of us to fulfill that role.

Romans 12:16 (NKJV) urges us to "be of the same mind." As believers, we are to put on the mind of Christ and work together to build His kingdom. This means unity is among the essentials of the faith and that with unity we receive God's power. When there is unity in the body, it thrives. This is beautifully pictured in the account of the early church in the book of Acts.

As the Holy Spirit continues to teach us reliance on one another, serving one another becomes a priority. We should focus on honor for and devotion to one another as we work together. We are called to accept one another, but we are also called to lovingly admonish one another in truth. We are called to bear with one another, to be patient and loving in our attitudes, to carry one another's burdens, and to encourage one another. Submission to one another out of love should be our driving motive in all we do.

As we mature in our faith and deepen our study of the Bible, God will reveal to us our tremendous need to consider the body of Christ as our family. Fellowship is vital to the church because we each depend on the others to help us grow in our faith and show a lost and dying world the love of Christ.

ACTION STEP:

In John 13:34–35; 15:12, 17, Jesus commanded believers to "love one another." Take time to read

Philippians with this thought in mind, and look up the "one another" verses in the books of Romans, Ephesians, Colossian, 1 Thessalonians, James, 1 Peter, and 1 John. Ask yourself how you can better apply these verses to your life in the next month. (You may find that the King James Version, the New King James Version, *and the* New American Standard Bible *will be the most helpful in this assignment.)*

FOR FURTHER READING:

Building Up One Another
Gene Getz

22
Submission

Likewise you younger people, submit yourselves to your elders. Yes, all of you be submissive to one another, and be clothed with humility, for "God resists the proud, but gives grace to the humble" (1 Peter 5:5 NKJV).

The twentieth century has been marked by great technological progress. New discoveries and advances have improved life, both in quality and quantity. There is no question that humankind has made great advances on many fronts. These advances in technology have been remarkable, but even more remarkable—and tragic—is the digression in the personal discipline that has marked the twentieth century.

One critically important personal discipline that has been eroded over the past few generations is that of submission. At all levels and in all arenas of life, submission has come under attack from those who resent being required to submit to anyone or anything. One example of this is the institution of marriage. God set up marriage as a covenant, which in this context is a sacred vow or oath taken before the Lord where both partners submit to one another for their mutual benefit. But what was intended as a blessing from God for couples has, for the majority of married men and women, eroded into a tragic and sad relationship. Selfishness and self-centeredness are the major reasons for the breakup of marriages. When couples join together in marriage without an attitude of submission, hard times are certain to come.

We can also see terrible consequences from the lack of submission to parental authority. Many families, including Christian families, reap the destructive consequences of children and teens not properly recognizing their parents' authority. But this sad situation doesn't stop at home. This lack of submission to parental authority spills over into our schools, and as these children grow, they take this rebelliousness into society in general. This translates into challenges in the workplace, where many employees resist authority whenever they can get away with it.

The lack of submission in these areas has had tragic consequences, but the most critical area where believers have fallen short is in submitting to the leading and teaching of the Holy Spirit. Far too often, believers live more like people of the world than as those who are devoted followers of Jesus Christ.

Our great example of submission is the Lord Jesus Christ Himself. His entire life was submitted to the leading of the Holy Spirit and to the will of His Father in heaven. Jesus was obedient, even though it ultimately meant that He, the only One who was perfectly holy and righteous, would become sin for us and be sacrificed to God so that we might be redeemed.

I believe that submission is one of the most difficult aspects of living a victorious Christian life. Yet without this discipline, we will enjoy very little real spiritual growth. Without submission, we can become like the branch that bears no fruit (John 15:5–8) or the salt that has lost its taste (Matthew 5:13), both of which are worthless to the cause of Christ.

ACTION STEP:

Think about the areas in your life where you need to work on the discipline of submission. Ask God to reveal these areas to you. Pray that God, through His Holy Spirit, will help you make progress in those areas.

FOR FURTHER READING:

A Heart for God
chapters 10 and 11, pp. 149–76
Sinclair B. Ferguson

23
Fasting

No, the kind of fasting I want calls you to free those who are wrongly imprisoned and to stop oppressing those who work for you. Treat them fairly and give them what they earn. I want you to share your food with the hungry and to welcome poor wanderers into your homes. Give clothes to those who need them, and do not hide from relatives who need your help. If you do these things, your salvation will come like the dawn. Yes, your healing will come quickly. Your godliness will lead you forward, and the glory of the LORD will protect you from behind (Isaiah 58:6–8).

Fasting is one of the important spiritual disciplines referred to in Scripture. It is also a practice that is beginning to make a comeback after what could be labeled a period of obscurity.

In the past few years, a number of good books on fasting have been written. Also, several evangelical leaders have become modern-day advocates for the practice. It is exciting to meet believers who have made fasting a part of their prayer and worship and to hear them talk about the impact fasting has had on their spiritual lives.

With this renewed interest in fasting, we should go to the Bible to see what it says about the practice and why we should seriously consider making it a part of our spiritual lives.

There are many references to fasting in the Scriptures. The Bible tells us that Moses, David, Daniel, Elijah, Esther, Ezra, Nehemiah, Paul, and the Lord Jesus

Himself all fasted at different times and for different reasons. These are examples of the right reasons and motivations for fasting. But there are also biblical examples of the wrong kinds of fasting—most notably, the kind the Pharisees and false teachers practiced during Jesus' time (Matthew 6:16).

What kind of fasting does God honor? Isaiah 58 provides an excellent contrast between false fasting and the type of fasting that pleases God. As with prayer and worship, the most important element of this discipline is proper purpose and motivation. It is also important to understand when we fast that we are being changed and transformed to the likeness of our Lord.

Another way fasting is like prayer is that there is no limit to the ways we can practice it. It can be as simple as skipping one meal, or it may involve omitting certain foods for a period. It can also involve a more aggressive approach, where the believer fasts for longer periods, such as one day, three days, or even a week.

A quick note: Not everyone should fast. There are legitimate medical reasons for not fasting, and if you have any doubts regarding your health, you should first seek medical advice before you begin fasting.

We should begin every fast in prayer to seek God's guidance. Also, we should have an objective behind every fast. The main objective in fasting is to receive an increased awareness of God and His will for our lives, but there are a variety of other reasons to fast. Lastly, fasting should be a private affair between you and God. When the believer follows these steps, fasting can be a strong force in his or her spiritual life.

ACTION STEP:

Read Isaiah 58 and meditate on what God is saying in this passage. Ask the Holy Spirit to guide you regarding fasting. Ask God when you should fast, for how long, and for what reason.

FOR FURTHER READING:

Fasting for Spiritual Breakthrough: A Guide to Nine Biblical Facts
Elmer L. Towns

24
Compassion

This is what the LORD Almighty says: Judge fairly and honestly, and show mercy and kindness to one another. Do not oppress widows, orphans, foreigners, and poor people. And do not make evil plans to harm each other (Zechariah 7:9–10).

My family has a Christmas tradition we hold dear as we celebrate the birth of our Savior: Every year we take time to watch videos of *It's a Wonderful Life,* the film starring Jimmy Stewart and produced by Frank Capra, and *A Christmas Carol,* the movie based on the short story by Charles Dickens.

Each of these films portrays a character whose life demonstrates the results of an existence without compassion. In *It's a Wonderful Life,* old man Potter, the stingy, rich villain of Bedford Falls, depicts in grand fashion how greed and covetousness can consume a person until even the slightest hint of conscience has been seared. Potter feeds his appetite for monetary wealth at the expense of others, using all sorts of trickery and deception. At the climax of the story, Potter thinks he has won as he watches the collapse of his longtime nemesis, George Bailey. But it is at this point that George Bailey's life demonstrates the reward of compassion and that friends and family are what really matter in life. To the believer, this movie can be a reminder of the truth of Galatians 6:7–8, that we truly do reap what we sow.

In *A Christmas Carol,* the main character is Ebenezer

Scrooge, whose life also teaches a profound truth regarding compassion. Throughout most of his life, the accumulation of wealth dominated Scrooge's thoughts and actions. As the years passed, this greed progressively worsened to the point that nothing was left but a cruel and harsh old man who was empty and alone with only thoughts of himself. Scrooge's response to the needs of others was either a sarcastic question or an attitude of total disdain. He saw the misfortunes of others as merely an inconvenience, and he clearly lacked even a speck of compassion, especially to those in greatest need.

The Scrooge character is a contrast to the Cratchit family, whose lives, even in the midst of a humble existence, exhibit the wonderful joy that kindness and compassion bring. Whether or not Dickens intended that it be so, the Cratchits are a demonstration of the biblical compassion that comes from a family's awareness of God's compassion toward them.

The climax of the story comes as Scrooge is transformed from a self-centered miser to a man overwhelmed with the spirit of compassion. It is always uplifting and moving to watch this transformation, and one cannot overlook the inference that can be made regarding the new birth and its results.

The Bible is clear that all believers need to display kindness and compassion for those around them. We are commanded to demonstrate the love of God to a lost world by caring for those in need. The Bible reminds us that when we show compassion in even the slightest way, we do it for the Lord.

It is a sad note that in many ways some nonbelievers display more compassion for those less fortunate than do many believers. As children of our loving and kind heavenly Father, we should work to be shining examples of compassion, both in word and in deed.

ACTION STEP:

Think about the needs of others around you and pray about how God would have you become involved in their lives. Then make a plan of action to meet those needs. Ask God to fill you with His compassion for those around you.

FOR FURTHER READING:

A Christmas Carol
Charles Dickens

25
Effective Prayer

Call to Me, and I will answer you, and I will tell you great and mighty things, which you do not know (Jeremiah 33:3 NASB).

I cannot remember a time in my life when I did not pray. I was taught to pray when I was a child, and from then until I had reached the age of thirty-six, few nights ever passed that I did not pray.

Most of the time, though, my prayers were short, self-centered, and, in retrospect, I believe, not effective. The first prayer I prayed that I am certain was effective was when I cried out, "God, help me!" It was the earnest prayer of a helpless person who had no hope left in himself. I know it was effective because at that moment God answered me with the greatest gift a lost sinner can have: being born again.

From that point on, I have been learning more and more about the wonderful privilege, power, and blessing of effective prayer. The Bible makes clear in the book of James that God acts on effective prayer. Effective prayer is the believer's communication with God, and it is one of the essentials to living an abundant life in Christ.

As with every element of the new life we enjoy as believers, effective prayer is possible only because we are allowed to approach a holy God through the person of Jesus Christ, the mediator between God and us. We can come to the Father in the name of Jesus Christ.

Our lives should represent the new covenant that the blood and body of our Lord made available to us.

There are some key fundamentals that will make us effective in our prayer lives. The first is that we ground ourselves in Scripture, which will assist and direct us in how we should pray. The more we learn of God through His Word, the more consistent our prayers will be with His will. Second, we need to pray in faith, which means that we approach God confident that He desires to listen to us and answer our prayers. This faith expresses our dependence on God and our confidence in His love for His children.

The third discipline necessary to have an effective prayer life relates to our daily walk as a disciple of Jesus Christ. The New Testament exhaustively instructs the believer in how to live. We have been called to a life of obedience that stems from our love for and gratitude to our Lord. When we are disobedient, we lose our ability to pray effectively. If we continue in disobedience, we can get to a point where we have very little sense of God whatsoever, and our prayers become less and less effective. As we lose focus on God, our minds are filled with the things of the world. Without repentance it is not possible to correct this condition. Repentance is vital to restore effective prayer, but I would add that even when we enjoy close fellowship with God, it is still necessary to confess our sins daily so that nothing is allowed to hinder our prayer.

Lastly, it is important that we forgive others, since God has forgiven us for so much (see Colossians 3:13). In Matthew 6:12–15, Jesus pointed out that forgiveness of those who sin against us is so important to the heavenly Father that it is a prerequisite for His hearing our prayers.

God has decreed effective prayer to be a mighty weapon in the building of His kingdom and in the lives of His children. Be sure that you are enjoying the blessing of effective prayer.

ACTION STEP:

Answer the following questions and make plans to take actions that will improve your life of prayer:

1. *How often do you pray?*
2. *What direct results have you witnessed from your prayers?*
3. *Do you have a specific time or place to pray?*
4. *Do you keep a list of your prayers?*
5. *What things can you do to improve your prayer life?*

FOR FURTHER READING:

How to Pray in the Spirit
chapters 1–10, pp. 15–56
John Bunyan

26
Discipleship

Therefore, go and make disciples of all the nations, baptizing them in the name of the Father and the Son and the Holy Spirit. Teach these new disciples to obey all the commands I have given you. And be sure of this: I am with you always, even to the end of the age (Matthew 28:19–20).

I recently saw this quotation of a Christian speaker: "I can think of no other time in history where the name of Jesus has been so frequently mentioned and yet the content of His life and teaching are so thoroughly ignored." This statement is an excellent point of reference as we analyze the topic of discipleship.

The most appropriate place to begin our consideration of discipleship is to thoughtfully read Matthew 28:18–20, where we see the Lord Jesus Christ's clear command for all believers to "go and make disciples." I believe this mandate clearly implies that if believers are to go and *make* disciples, then they need to understand what it takes to *be* a disciple. More importantly, this means that we should live as true disciples live—not just in title, but in deeds.

Discipleship is the process by which a believer receives the opportunity and encouragement to grow to full potential for God's plan for his or her life. Unfortunately, many who come to a true saving faith fail to receive the solid discipling God desires for new believers. Furthermore, the failure to properly disciple new believers leads to a weaker church body, which leads to weakness in other individual believers.

In order to be an effective disciple of Jesus Christ, it is essential that you have a solid doctrinal foundation from the Word, a regular discipline of Bible reading and study, and a daily special time with your Lord. It is critical that you continually walk in the power of the Holy Spirit.

As you continue to grow, you will be able to follow Jesus' command to "make disciples." Then it will be time to pray that God will bring others into your life you can disciple.

As you begin to work at discipling another believer, keep some basic steps in mind. The first step in discipling someone is to recognize that a new believer needs assurance. Every new convert needs to know that he or she has truly been born again. This step confirms that a believer is truly regenerated.

Also keep in mind that new believers yearn to be accepted and loved. Like infants at birth, new believers are vulnerable, at times demanding, and quite often not in true control of themselves spiritually. What they require most of all is love and attention.

It is also important to remember that new believers may need protection from a variety of negative influences, such as cults or false teachers. They also should be encouraged to seek a church where they can receive loving and sound teaching. Just as natural babies require physical nourishment to grow, new believers require good spiritual food on a regular basis so they can grow. This is why Bible reading and study is so vital—without it there will be little growth.

Lastly, new believers need to be taught and trained in the art of living a life that is pleasing to the Lord. This can be done through the development of the spiritual disciplines—such as prayer, fasting, and Bible study—as directed and led by the Holy Spirit. This process will ensure that the believer maintains a growing fellowship with Christ.

ACTION STEP:

Ask yourself if you need someone to disciple you. If so, pray and ask God to lead you to someone who might be open to this involvement. If you don't need to be discipled, ask yourself if you could disciple another believer. If so, ask God if He has someone He wants you to work with.

FOR FURTHER READING:

The Lost Art of Disciple Making
chapters 5 and 6, pp. 59–82
Leroy Eims

Section 5

A WATCHFUL LIFE

27

The Fear of God

And remember that the heavenly Father to whom you pray has no favorites when he judges. He will judge or reward you according to what you do. So you must live in reverent fear of him during your time as foreigners here on earth (1 Peter 1:17).

I would submit that most people have no real comprehension of what the term *the fear of God* means or what relevance it has in our lives today. I would also submit that at the beginning of the twentieth century, almost everyone knew what the fear of God was and why they needed to have that fear. One of the foundational problems of our society today is that we as a people have little regard for almighty God, let alone a fear of Him.

There are many references in the Bible to the fear of God. In fact, the Scriptures place great importance on this reverential awe of God and the need to cultivate it in our hearts on a daily basis. The book of Proverbs, which is regarded as one of the most practical books of Scripture, provides a clear presentation of what it means to fear God and the benefits believers derive from this proper fear of Him.

There are a number of verses in the Bible that remind us that the lack of this fear is at the root of wickedness. On the positive side, however, the biblical meaning of the fear of God starts with our realization of who the triune God is and our recognition of His wondrous attributes. When we begin to lay hold of these things, we should be overwhelmed with the kind of fear that produces awe, reverence, and worship for our God. This sense of awe will drive us to a never ending love and adoration for our heavenly Father, our Lord Jesus Christ, and the blessed Holy Spirit.

In the book of Proverbs it states: "The fear of the LORD is the beginning of wisdom" (9:10 NKJV). If we want wisdom, we need to start with a reverential fear of God. If we lack wisdom, the first thing we should do is examine our hearts to see if this sense of awe for God fills our hearts. Proverbs also tells us that the fear of the Lord will keep us from sinning (16:6), lead us to a life of satisfaction (19:23), and, when combined with humility, lead to riches and honor and long life (22:4).

As I researched the topic of the fear of God, I was struck by the fact that Jesus Christ Himself feared the Lord. Isaiah 11:2–3 (NASB), one of the prophecies forecasting the coming of the Messiah, reveals that not only does Jesus fear the Lord, but that "He will *delight* in the fear of the LORD."

Every believer would do well to note what the Bible says about the fear of God and follow the example of the Lord Jesus Christ, who delighted in the fear of God. A clear and correct understanding of what it is to properly fear God will play a large part in our living the transformed life we are called to live.

ACTION STEP:

Look up the fourteen verses in Proverbs that refer to the fear of the Lord and write them down so you can remind yourself of the importance of fearing Him. Take note of the benefits we derive from fearing God and the consequences we face if we don't.

FOR FURTHER READING:

The Joy of Fearing God
Jerry Bridges

28
Deceptive Faith

Not all people who sound religious are really godly. They may refer to me as "Lord," but they still won't enter the Kingdom of Heaven. The decisive issue is whether they obey my Father in heaven (Matthew 7:21).

When I was young, one of my favorite activities was hiking in the mountains. During one of my outings, an event occurred that left a lasting impression on me.

Two of my friends and I began a hike across a mountain that was part of a small range. We started out from a valley and worked our way up through a thick forest. Thinking we were progressing toward our goal, we continually talked about how we were making progress. But after hiking a few hours we ended up very close to where we had started. That's right! We had gone in a complete circle. We could not believe it!

All three of us were sure of our positions and that we were making progress, yet in reality we were all fooled, deceived, and lost. We were so confident in our own abilities as hikers that we made the mistake of not using a compass. Fortunately, other than a few wasted hours and some embarrassment, we suffered no real loss that day.

There was, however, another experience that left an even deeper mark on my life. It was the experience of being spiritually lost when I truly believed I had found the way to salvation.

When I was seven years old, I responded to an altar call at a church service. I was too shy to go forward, but I silently asked Jesus to come into my heart. From that point on, I believed I was "saved."

I continued to attend church, rarely missed praying at night, and even tried to learn Bible verses. I really believed my life was pleasing to God. In reality, though, the things I did that I thought pleased God made little difference in my life. By the time I reached high school, my lifestyle was more consistent with the world than with the Bible. Yet I never doubted that I had been saved.

I met the woman who would be my wife while we were both in high school. Her "salvation" experience was similar to mine. We went to church together, and we had a good understanding of the Christian faith. We got married while we were in college and continued to go to church together. I was even baptized in the small church we attended.

As time went by, however, our busy schedules kept us from going to church consistently. It was not until after the birth of our first child that we returned to church on a regular basis. By the time our second child was born, we were active attendees, participating in the church and in Bible study. If you had asked us if we had saving faith in Jesus Christ, our answer would have been a resounding "Absolutely!"

But something was missing in our lives. Without knowing it, we were spiritually lost. We knew *about* Jesus, but we really didn't *know Him.* For twenty-nine years, I had lived a life of what I call "deceptive faith." I had put my trust in a childhood memory, believing that little prayer I uttered would keep me from going to hell. I lived what I believed was a Christian life. My life was a lot like those of many around me, including my wife's. I compared how I lived with how others lived, and I drew confidence from the fact that my conduct was better than theirs.

I had owned a Bible since I was six years old and had added other copies of the Word to my collection. In reality, though, I rarely read it, except at church. To me, the Bible was a just symbol. I knew I should be reading it, but I never got much out of it when I did.

All this changed on October 12, 1980, when I realized for the first time how terribly deceived I had been and that I had been lost—headed in the wrong direction without a compass. I could see how blinded I had been to the truth. That day I was born to a new life in Jesus Christ. I knew I had been changed. I immediately was drawn to start reading the Bible. The words were so clear, so obvious, that I wondered why I hadn't seen them this way before.

I began to understand what the Bible reveals about saving faith and the warning that many are like I was: on the broad road that leads to hell, not on the narrow way to heaven. I discovered there is only one compass that leads to heaven, and that is the Bible, which directs our paths to Jesus Christ.

It has been almost twenty years since that event, and I have never forgotten the fear that hit me as I reflected about how deceived I had been and how much I had rested on a false hope. It is for that reason that I continue to encourage professing believers to examine their faith to see if it is real. Go to the only standard that matters—the Bible. Be sure you are not resting in deceptive faith.

ACTION STEP:

Examine the faith that you are resting on and make sure that it is the kind the Bible reveals as saving faith. Ask God to illuminate the words as you read. Ask Him to show you where you are really at in your relationship with Him.

FOR FURTHER READING:

The Beginnings: Word and Spirit in Conversation
Paul Helm

29
Idolatry

Take heed to yourselves, lest your heart be deceived, and you turn aside and serve other gods and worship them (Deuteronomy 11:16 NKJV*).*

I should not be surprised if some readers wonder why I am including the topic of idolatry in this book. That is because many believers would not consider idolatry a relevant topic for today.

To most Christians today, the word *idolatry* conjures up images of ancient carvings that, for the most part, have long since been discarded. Their thoughts go back to the Old Testament accounts of the struggles of the children of Israel with idol worship and of the pagan nations that regularly worshiped idols.

However, I would assert that idolatry is very commonplace today, even in the church, and that it is one of the leading causes of weakness and distraction among believers, as well as the lack of strong focus on evangelism and outreach.

One definition of the word *idol* is "an object of extreme devotion." The principle meaning of the word *idolatry* is "the worship of a physical object as a god." Using these definitions, I would submit that a sizable portion of the populations of North America, Europe, and the Pacific Rim are consumed with different forms of idolatry. I believe that our modern culture may well be the most idolatrous in history, simply because we have so much that can capture our affections.

The idols of today do not fit our concept of what an

idol is supposed to look like. But idols can be things that are in and of themselves necessary or things that bring casual enjoyment. Let's examine some modern-day idols that plague our lives. One example of this in contemporary society is that of success. Hard work and successful careers are not evil in and of themselves. But in our culture we have a lust to "have it all" and to show everyone that we have "made it." We have a preoccupation with attaining status and the acceptance and applause of others, at almost any cost.

We also idolize entertainment. We crave spectator sports, our three hundred TV channels, and our all-night video stores. Like success in the world of work, entertainment in and of itself is neither good nor bad. It is when these things become objects of "extreme devotion" that we fall into idolatry.

The list of things that could become idols is extensive, but I believe the most worshiped idol of all is *self*. We make ourselves idols when we become the objects of our own extreme devotion. The greatest preoccupation of people today, including many believers, is the worship of self. This obsession with self has been a great part of our loss of the vision of who God is and how He should be the object of worship and devotion for every believer.

The first step to recapturing devotion to God and the proper worship of Him is to ask Him to reveal anything that has become an idol. When God brings those things to our attention, we will need to make adjustments in the way we approach those things that have become idols for us. We also need to increase the time we spend in prayer and Bible study. For some, this will be like exploring new ground.

Remember how easy it is to turn something into an idol. Work to honor the first two commandments. Keep God at the center of everything.

ACTION STEP:

Ask God to reveal to you things or activities that may have become idols and keep you from focusing on Him. Be honest with yourself and ask for the strength to change.

FOR FURTHER READING:

God in the Wasteland
chapter 5, pp. 88–117
David F. Wells

30
Worldliness

Love not the world, neither the things that are in the world (1 John 2:15 KJV).

Anyone who has ever had a clogged kitchen faucet has had to do one of two things: take apart the faucet and clean the filter himself or have someone else do this task. It is amazing to see the difference in the water flow after the filter is cleared of the sediment that has accumulated over time. This is especially true in areas of the country where there has been an increase in hard water.

The clogging action of sediment in a faucet filter is a lot like the clogging action of worldliness in the minds of believers and prevents them from receiving a healthy flow of the living water from God's Word and the Holy Spirit. As in the example of the filter, the more that sediment accumulates in the heart and mind, the less likely it will be that truth gets through. Believers can gradually become loaded down with worldliness to the point where they have very little influence for God. I suspect this is the condition of many believers today.

It is very important that we believers understand what worldliness is and how it can gain strongholds in our lives. To be worldly is to be engrossed in and devoted to this present world and to the things it pursues and values.

Like all sin, worldliness has its beginning in our minds. How we think will ultimately determine how we act, and what we think about is a reflection of our hearts and wills. And when we are worldly, we lose interest in the things of the Word of God.

The mental framework from which we process information is called our *worldview.* Everyone has a worldview. Believers are either strengthening their biblical worldview or being drawn toward a secular worldview, which leads them to become increasingly more worldly. If your worldview is strongly influenced by the Word of God, you will process information and events from a biblical perspective. But if your worldview is a secular one, you will process information and events through the filter of human wisdom.

As we begin to understand this fundamental truth, we can easily see how a believer can be enticed away from God and into the things of this world. We can comprehend how some believers become like the world around them.

The Bible warns that loving the world can distract a person and rob him or her of the chance for true saving faith in the Savior. In the parable of the sower, Christ likens the Word of God to seeds that fall among the thorns and are eventually choked out. In that case, Christ tells us, the seed of God's Word fails to take root because of the cares of this world, and there is spiritual death.

The fourth chapter of the book of James offers a hard-hitting contrast between those who draw close to God and those who remain close to the world: "You adulterers! Don't you realize that friendship with this world makes you an enemy of God? I say it again, that if your aim is to enjoy this world, you can't be a friend of God" (James 4:4). James also tells us in the same chapter to withstand the world's attractiveness. But how do we do that? First, we need to stay humble before God. We also need to resist the devil and his influence and grow close to God. We need to realize how dependent we are on God, and we need to invest daily in building our relationship with Him.

God has promised that if we are faithful in this process that He will empower us by the Holy Spirit to overcome the world, just as our Lord did during His life and ministry on this earth.

ACTION STEP:

Make a list of the things you think pull you toward the world. Be honest with yourself. Ask God to give you strength in resisting the lures Satan has set up for you. Make a commitment to be a "friend of God" and not a "friend of the world."

FOR FURTHER READING:

Personal Holiness in Times of Temptation
chapter 3, pp. 55–78
Bruce H. Wilkinson

31
Materialism

And he said to them, "Take heed, and beware of all covetousness; for a man's life does not consist in the abundance of his possessions" (Luke 12:15 RSV*).*

In his book *Financial Freedom,* author Ray Linder tells two stories that epitomize both the curse and the blessing of wealth. The stories are of two great legends of success in the early part of the twentieth century, F. W. Woolworth, the founder of the Woolworth five-and-ten-cent stores, and Milton S. Hershey, founder of the Hershey chocolate company.

Both of these men amassed great fortunes. But the way they used their money provides a classic contrast between the preoccupation with the accumulation of wealth (one form of materialism) and the recognition that wealth affords opportunities to provide for others. The legacy of both men reminds us of the consequences of selfishness and the rewards that come to those with generous hearts. The story of F. W. Woolworth and his family reads like a great tragedy, whereas Milton Hershey's legacy of service to others continues in his family and business to this day.

We believers need to learn that our attitude toward material things says a lot about where we are spiritually. Much of the world places more value on things than people, but as believers we should make certain we don't follow that path. God examines the motives of our hearts and watches how we use the material blessings He has given us. We need to clearly understand the responsibility of stewardship and the impact it should have on our daily lives. (See chapter 21, "Stewardship," in *Basics for Believers,* volume 1.)

The abundance of *stuff*—material things competing for our attention—in our world today makes it more important than ever for us to involve God in our daily decisions about how we use our wealth. We are continually faced with the option of spending our money to acquire something of temporal value or of using it to gain something of eternal value by giving to someone in need or to a ministry for the building of the kingdom of God.

The Bible provides helpful insights and instructions on how to avoid being ensnared by materialism. For one thing, the Word points out that material possessions are temporary and that we will not take our things with us when we die (1 Timothy 6:7). In fact, God may choose to remove them from us even sooner.

God has given us money not just to provide for our needs, but also to help us see where our values really are. The Bible says that the way we use our money will demonstrate who we really serve. The Scriptures caution that the love of money and the things that money may bring is at the root of evil (1 Timothy 6:10).

We know that the preoccupation with money can cause a person to be untruthful or damage that person's character. But the love of money and possessions can do something even more serious: take our focus off God.

The world is in love with money and the things that it can provide. Many in our government think money will solve all our social problems as demonstrated by the amont of money spent—and wasted—on welfare.

Believers, on the other hand, should love God first and commit themselves to avoiding what the Bible calls "the lust of the eyes" (1 John 2:16 KJV). We should long to serve others with the things God has given us, and we should be faithful stewards of God's gifts.

ACTION STEP:

Take stock of all the material things God has given you. Then ask yourself how you can better use those things for the benefit of others and the glory of God.

FOR FURTHER READING:

Financial Freedom
chapters 1 and 2, pp. 15–45
Ray Linder

32
Temptation

No temptation has overtaken you that is not common to man. God is faithful, and he will not let you be tempted beyond your strength, but with the temptation will also provide the way of escape, that you may be able to endure it (1 Corinthians 10:13 RSV*).*

There are three sources of temptation that will be part of believers' lives until they are ushered into eternity: the *world* and all it offers, the *flesh* (that unredeemed part of our nature), and the *devil* and his great force of fallen angels.

It is vitally important for believers to understand these three areas of temptation and their corresponding evil desires: "The lust of the flesh, and the lust of the eyes, and the pride of life" (1 John 2:16 KJV). That is so because our enemy, Satan, knows how to use them so that they appear harmless to us. Gaining an understanding of how subtle and seemingly innocent temptation can be is critical if we are to have the victory God has made possible through the gifts of the believer's instruction book for life, the Bible, and the Holy Spirit.

I have already addressed the *world* and all it offers in chapter 30 of this book, "Worldliness." Of the three areas of temptation, the love of the world (which is related to "the lust of the eyes . . . and the pride of life") can be the most subtle and seemingly innocent. That is because so much of what the world offers is not inherently evil. But the devil can take that which is in and of itself not sinful and make it that way. For example, there is nothing evil about wanting to own a comfortable, nice house. However, sin can enter this picture when our motives behind purchasing a particular home are wrong. Since the late fifties, the average single-family house in America has more than doubled in size, and yet the size of the average family has declined. It appears that materialism, the lust for "more," plays a huge part in which homes we choose to buy.

As believers, how do we decide when our desire for a comfortable home crosses the line and becomes materialism? How do we balance our own comfort with the needs of others? How much does the lust of the eye play in our decision? These are not simple questions, and there could be a multitude of answers to them. The bottom line is that believers need to make sure they are not more influenced by the standards of the world than by the commands of the Scriptures.

When we talk about the *flesh* (related to "the lust of the flesh" in 1 John 2:16, but also to the "pride of life"), we are talking about the old nature that makes a believer vulnerable to sinful passions and attitudes. This area of temptation is focused on God-given natural inclinations that we allow to become perverted by sin. For example, one of the most wonderful gifts from God for a married couple is that of sex. But this gift is debased when it becomes nothing more than lust and evil passion. In that case, it becomes sin that ultimately leads to destruction. Another example is the desire to succeed. Goal-setting and creativity are gifts from God, but if we allow egotism and greed to distort those gifts, they can consume and destroy us.

The *devil* and his vast members of fallen angels work within our thoughts and attitudes. Our minds are the devil's great playground. He constantly opposes God's work in the lives of Christians. Here are just a few examples: God wants us to grow in humility, but Satan feeds our pride. God commands us to think on good things, but Satan continually reminds us of failure, evil desires, and sinful thoughts. God desires that we be transformed by the renewing of our minds from His truth, but Satan feeds us with lies and destructive thoughts meant to keep us from growing.

As we come to understand different sources of temptation, it is reassuring to know that God has provided a way out. We need to remember that the Holy Spirit within us is stronger than those roots of temptation. We can be more than conquerors in our battle with temptation. We should be more like our Lord, who was tempted in all ways, yet was without sin.

ACTION STEP:

Think about how you have been tempted recently. Then write down those temptations. Record what you think was the source of the temptations and what your response was. Memorize Hebrews 2:18 and ask God to help you discern and resist temptation.

FOR FURTHER READING:

Not Good If Detached
chapter 3, pp. 27–45
Corrie ten Boom

33
Anger

In your anger do not sin: Do not let the sun go down while you are still angry, and do not give the devil a foothold (Ephesians 4:26–27 NIV).

As a parent, one of the greatest gifts you can give your children is to teach them how to handle anger biblically and constructively. This will give your children an extraordinary advantage in the pursuit of success in most areas of life, starting with family relationships and continuing into school life, social relationships, and the workplace. More important, the ability to handle anger correctly will play out in their marriages and provide them with the ability to teach these principles to their own children.

One of the great tragedies in our culture is people's failure to understand what anger is, how to properly manage it, and how to use it as the Creator intended. We can see the results of this all around us. Uncontrolled and destructive anger has become a serious problem in many areas of our society.

In the book *The Other Side of Love*, Gary Chapman deals instructively with this issue. Chapman gives the reader a clear overview of anger, where it comes from, and what its purposes are. Then he discusses ways that will help a person learn the biblical way to process anger. Unless you are one of those rare persons who has already learned how to properly handle anger, this book should be on the "absolute read" list. Here is a quotation from the first chapter:

> Anger is not evil; anger is not sinful; anger is not a part of our fallen nature; anger is not Satan at work in our lives. Quite the contrary. Anger is evidence that we are made in God's image; it demonstrates that we still have some concern for justice and righteousness in spite of our fallen estate.

It is quite a revelation for many that rather than try to rid ourselves of anger, we should be thankful for the capacity to become angry.

Chapman says that the first step in processing anger in a productive way is to learn to recognize that you are angry and to accept the reality of that emotion. The next step—in many ways, this is the most important—is to refrain from what would be your normal response, stop and think about what the issue or offense is that produced the anger, and then think about the response options you have. Then you can work out a resolution in a constructive way.

Another section of *The Other Side of Love* deals with how to recognize and deal with distorted anger. Unfortunately, much of the anger we see in our world today is distorted anger. It comes from incorrectly perceiving wrongdoing when in fact there was none, or when we believe we have the facts when in fact we do not.

If we are truly committed to becoming mature disciples of Jesus Christ, we must learn how to properly handle anger. We must ask God to reveal the sinful ways we handle anger—whether we tend to explode or implode (turn our anger inward and allow it to come out in destructive ways)—and learn by the power of the Holy Spirit to prevent this from occurring.

ACTION STEP:

Write down the areas where you think you are most vulnerable to distorted anger. Start by thinking about things that have made you angry recently. Ask God to help you to change this process.

FOR FURTHER READING:

The Other Side of Love
Gary Chapman

Section 6

AN ORGANIZED LIFE

34
Common Sense

The godly give good advice, but fools are destroyed by their lack of common sense (Proverbs 10:21).

I recently read a magazine article that reinforced the idea that opportunities continue to be available in America for anyone willing to work. One statement in the article jumped out at me: "It is much easier to earn an honest living in America than it is to earn a dishonest one." In other words, it takes more work in the long run to be dishonest than it does to be honest. The same rule applies in speaking the truth: It is much less taxing to be honest than it is to exert the energy and effort required to be dishonest.

Another reality I have observed is that it is much easier to be busy than it is to be lazy. If you don't believe that, just observe how hard some people work just to avoid working hard.

More truth: Never spend more than you earn, and save some of what you earn. Fifty years ago, this point would have been too obvious to need stating, but today it needs to be made.

What do all these things have in common? Simply that they are examples of what we call "common sense." They are all things that, if we just stop and think about them, are fairly obvious pieces of wisdom.

Sadly, a great many people in our culture today lack common sense in many areas of their lives. That leads us to some key questions: What has happened to common sense? Why do so few people have or use common sense? What is our greatest source of common sense?

I believe that a major reason for the loss of common sense in a sizable portion of our population is our tendency to overlook and discount the Word of God, the Bible. Common sense is a gift from God, and many of its elements are spelled out in the Bible. As people become disconnected from the Scriptures, they become disconnected from the wisdom of God.

Those who choose not to search and apply the Word of God to their lives lose out on many sound, time-tested, and valuable directives. When we throw away the foundations of common sense found in the Bible, we find ourselves in a vacuum that will be filled with the wisdom of the world and of the natural man, and this leads to destruction.

Webster's Collegiate Dictionary defines common sense as "sound and prudent but often unsophisticated judgment." The world is captivated by the sophisticated, but in many ways it has abandoned the sound and the prudent.

If you desire to have common sense and let it impact your life, go to the Bible and discover the treasure of wisdom within its pages.

ACTION STEP:

Read Proverbs 22 and write down its "common sense" principles. Think about how you might apply these principles to your life.

FOR FURTHER READING:

Something New Under the Sun: Ancient Wisdom for Contemporary Living
Ray Pritchard

35

Setting Priorities

And she had a sister called Mary, who also sat at Jesus' feet and heard His word. But Martha was distracted with much serving, and she approached Him and said, "Lord, do You not care that my sister has left me to serve alone? Therefore tell her to help me." And Jesus answered and said to her, "Martha, Martha, you are worried and troubled about many things. But one thing is needed, and Mary has chosen that good part, which will not be taken away from her" (Luke 10:39–42 NKJV).

The year 2000 will mark some special anniversaries in my life. One is my celebration for having been involved in the world of work for forty years. Far more important to me than that is the observance of thirty-five years of marriage for my wife and me. Without question, however, my most important anniversary of the year 2000 will be the commemoration of twenty years since I came to a saving faith in the Lord Jesus Christ.

Each of these life experiences has played a major role in who I am as a person and has provided the opportunity for me to learn and grow—through successes and failures as well as triumphs and tragedies.

One lesson that has played a significant role in every area of my life—and a lesson I learned the hard way—is the necessity of setting priorities. There are tremendous benefits to understanding and mastering the principle of priority setting, whether it involves the spiritual life, marriage, family, school, work, or any other area of life. On the other hand, a lack of mastery of this discipline will be costly.

I have made reference to three areas of my own life—my work, marriage, and relationship with God—so I could provide some examples of my own development in understanding the value of establishing priorities.

When I was sixteen I worked in the construction business as a laborer. I had the good fortune to work with a group of workers who taught me the value of organizing my work in a way that maximized my output while minimizing my efforts. They also taught me to set things in order of importance so that I could complete the most important aspect of the overall work first. In short, I learned to work smart, not just hard. These lessons have served me well, and I remain grateful to those who taught me these basics.

Unfortunately, I did not apply these principles to my studies during my college years, and I suffered the consequences of failing to set good priorities. In retrospect, I realize I made my college life much more difficult because I failed to apply the principle of priority setting.

I also saw the repercussions of not establishing priorities in the early years of my marriage. My wife and I were both guilty of not making God our first priority. Don't misunderstand—we were very "religious." We attended church and had all the outward trappings of being "good Christian" people. But God was not the center of our lives. We also found ourselves putting the interests of self over the welfare of our relationship. Over time, these mistakes were very costly and nearly resulted in the disintegration of our home and marriage.

It was around that time that God taught us a great

lesson about priorities. In October of 1980, my wife and I both came to a saving faith in the Lord Jesus Christ. At that moment, God clearly showed us His priorities and how far from them we had really been.

As God began to transform our lives, we learned that our top priority was to glorifiy and love God and to study and love His Word. We also placed priority on our love for one another and on raising our children in the fear and admonition of the Lord. We made sharing our faith with others and our witness in the conduct of our daily lives a priority. We began to learn the importance of worship, prayer, study, and giving.

As God blessed us in our learning process, He allowed trials and testing. But through the years we have seen the wonderful blessing of living lives that reflect biblical priorities.

ACTION STEP:

Write down answers to the following questions. Then ask God how you should adjust your priorities:

1. *Have I truly made God my top priority?*
2. *Do my priorities reflect a biblical foundation?*
3. *Where are areas in which my priorities are not in order?*

FOR FURTHER READING:

Been There. Done That. Now What? The Meaning of Life May Surprise You
chapter 9, pp. 147–63
Ed Young

36
Success

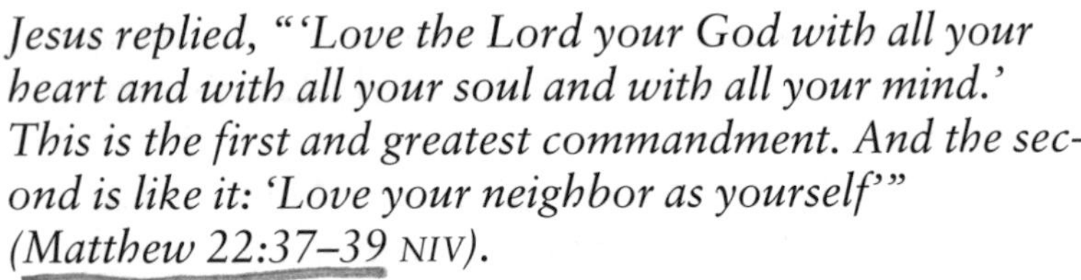

Jesus replied, "'Love the Lord your God with all your heart and with all your soul and with all your mind.' This is the first and greatest commandment. And the second is like it: 'Love your neighbor as yourself'" (Matthew 22:37–39 NIV*).*

My parents lived through the Great Depression of the 1930s and were profoundly marked by that experience. Because they both came from poor families, this time was especially difficult, and it left a lifelong attitude that affected most aspects of their lives. They came out of this ordeal with a strong work ethic and a real desire, in a worldly sense, to improve the quality of life and to become "successful." I was influenced by this mind-set and, as an adult, embraced their vision of success with determination and drive.

My parents were not unique, nor was I. This attitude was dominant in the culture in the decades following the 1930s. Most people wanted to achieve the American Dream, and much of this dream translated into the term *success*—materially, financially, socially, and environmentally. *Prosperity, growth,* and *opportunity* were commonly heard words throughout the subsequent five decades.

As we begin a new millennium, much of what we see today in our culture is a reflection of what started as a result of the Great Depression and the aftermath of World War II. There has never been greater opportunity for success, and as a nation most of us are better off materially and financially than ever before. But this success has come at a great price. Sadly, there is less and less emphasis all the time on the biblical truth and moral character that once played prominent roles in our society.

Many individuals and families have truly achieved that great goal of the American Dream only to awaken to a nightmare. Financial success has not provided peace to their hearts. Material things have not produced true contentment. The "toys" of this age have not replaced the need for relationships, friendships, and inner fulfillment. We are a people who have placed God on the periphery. For many of us, the Bible is just a decorative item that serves as a spiritual prop on special occasions or as a symbol on our coffee tables.

Working hard and using the gifts and abilities God has given us is worthwhile. The desire to improve our standard of life is a reasonable goal. But when these things replace God at the center of our being, then we are moving in the wrong direction. We believers must resist this ever-present temptation to become like the world around us. We need to turn away from embracing the world's desires and preoccupations.

We are called to look at life differently from the way the world does. As Christians, we have been told what the secret of life is, and it is this: We are made to glorify God with all that we are and to enjoy Him forever.

Success for the believer is to know God more and more and to grow in enjoyment of Him. The more we know Him, the better we know and understand ourselves. As our knowledge of God increases, we are enabled to love God with all of our hearts, with all of our souls, all of our strength, and all of our minds, and to love our neighbors as ourselves. As we do this, we fulfill that for which God created us.

ACTION STEP:

Go to a library or pick up a copy of the Shorter Catechism *(sometimes called the* Westminster Shorter Catechism*), and read and note questions one, two, three, forty-two, and eighty-five. Also, think about your own ideas of "success." Think about how they line up with God's Word.*

FOR FURTHER READING:

The Shorter Catechism with Scripture Proofs
The Banner of Truth Trust

37

Practice

But one thing I do: Forgetting what is behind and straining toward what is ahead, I press on toward the goal to win the prize for which God has called me heavenward in Christ Jesus (Philippians 3:13–14 NIV*).*

History records the names of many famous people whose speeches inspired millions. One such person was Winston Churchill, who, many historians would agree, made a greater impact through his speeches than almost anyone else during World War II. Most people have seen newsreels of some of his famous oratory, and I have personally heard people quote Churchill's now-famous speeches.

What many people do not realize, however, is that giving speeches did not come easily to Churchill. The story has been told that he actually tended to stutter, so in order for him to deliver an excellent speech, he had to go over the material again and again for many hours.

Practice is also necessary for success in the area of sports. We have all watched as gifted athletes perform spectacular feats. If you read the biographies of most sports legends, you will be amazed at the amount of practice it takes for them to be the very best they can be. Practice for the athlete means investing incredible amounts of time and energy in the sport and being intensely focused on a goal. Coaches recognize the importance of practice and how a good series of practices can have a positive effect on a team's performance.

Another area where practice is critical is in the military services. The military has long understood that victory in battle depends upon the ability of soldiers to carry out their assigned responsibilities, even under extremely adverse conditions. In the military, training is often in the form of repetition. Servicemen repeat the same drills until they can perform them almost instinctively. Without the intensity and focus, without the repetition, without following orders even to the most minute detail, the servicemen would never master split-second reactions in crucial situations.

For even the most gifted people, great performances in all endeavors almost never take place without practice. For many speakers, like Winston Churchill, practice is the only way to overcome limitations. For athletes, practice hones the skills he or she already possesses. For those in the military, practice is preparation for overcoming life-and-death crises.

Practice can be hard work, and that is why many have a difficult time putting effort into it. Many start out well but lose their commitment over time and end up not reaching their full potential. Some fail to grasp the importance of practice and the impact it has on how they perform. But practice is essential for success, even in the spiritual arena.

In the New Testament, the apostle Paul lays out the many aspects of living the Christian life, and he reminds us to be diligent in the practice of these various disciplines. As soldiers in the army of God, we are called to be faithful in following the orders of our Captain. As the Holy Spirit leads and directs us and as we develop our skills through practice, we grow and produce fruit.

ACTION STEP:

Pick out one spiritual discipline in your life—prayer, Scripture reading, fasting—in which you wish to improve. Make a commitment to practice regularly until you reach that goal. Ask God to empower you through His Spirit. Keep track of your progress, using a journal or a simple notepad.

FOR FURTHER READING:

Alive for the First Time
chapters 8 and 9, pp. 151–93
David C. Needham

38

Self-Control and Endurance

Knowing God leads to self-control. Self-control leads to patient endurance, and patient endurance leads to godliness (2 Peter 1:6).

As we read and study the New Testament, we begin to comprehend more and more the meaning of being a true believer and of a life of faith in the risen Christ.

The first chapter of 2 Peter provides an excellent summary of the importance of living out our faith and of growing in the knowledge of the Lord. Verse 6 is a key to this passage: "Knowing God leads to self-control. Self-control leads to patient endurance, and patient endurance leads to godliness." This verse makes clear that if we are to become what God desires us to be, then we need to know God. And knowing Him will lead to patience, self-control, and endurance.

Getting to know God is the first step referred to in 2 Peter 1:6, but we need to understand that knowing God means far more than acknowledging facts we learn from the Scriptures. Peter tells us that with a true knowledge of God, which is possible only with the help of the Holy Spirit, comes the divine power necessary to live a godly life. This monumental point concerning our sanctification will profoundly change the way we live.

It is only possible to live as we have been commanded to live if we are growing in the true knowledge of God and are receiving the supernatural power necessary to live in a Christlike manner. It is precisely this power that allows believers to develop control over the fleshly nature and to live in obedience by walking in the Spirit and obeying His guidance.

As we grow in self-control, victory over sin becomes a pattern in our lives. Yes, there will still be struggles and occasional failures, but as we learn self-control, sin becomes the exception and not the rule. And as the believer grows in self-control, he or she responds more and more to the leadings of the Holy Spirit in the areas of Bible study, prayer, acts of kindness, giving, and rejoicing with thanksgiving. This self-control, which is derived from that miraculous power of God, distinguishes true believers from those who don't know God.

As we become stronger in our self-control, God will allow hardship and adversity to play a larger role in our lives. It is under those circumstances that we develop endurance and where the life of the believer so clearly displays the strength and witness of the Holy Spirit.

Endurance is simply the ability to remain firm in God in the face of temptation or adversity. Endurance means standing firm to what God calls you to do in spite of sinful and destructive behavior in your mate or a family member. Endurance means not responding in a sinful way when you are falsely accused and your reputation damaged or destroyed.

As self-control and endurance become our first inclination, our lives will demonstrate true godliness. We will be conformed to the image of Christ because we are being made holy.

ACTION STEP:

Write out in one or two sentences the key elements that I have discussed regarding self-control and endurance. Thoughtfully read 2 Peter 1:1–10, noting Peter's instruction in verse 10 to "work hard to prove that you really are among those God has called and chosen."

FOR FURTHER READING:

The Forgotten Blessing
chapters 6, 7, and 8, pp. 67–105
Henry Holloman

39

Spiritual Gifts

Do not neglect the spiritual gift within you (1 Timothy 4:14 NASB*).*

I believe one of the least understood doctrines of the New Testament is that of spiritual gifts. Many believers have no idea what spiritual gifts are. Others have a basic understanding of this important doctrine, yet don't recognize their own area of giftedness. No wonder so many churches lack people to serve in various roles!

Two things are certain when believers fail to recognize and use their spiritual gifts. First, they will never fully realize their own potential in service to God. Second, the church will be deprived of some valuable giftedness and talent.

If we are to fully realize our potential in building up God's kingdom, then we need to understand the area of spiritual gifts. We need to understand what they are, and we need to find out how God has gifted each of us individually.

Spritual gifts are the skills or abilities the Lord gives each believer that equip that person to effectively perform a function in the body of Christ. We need to remember that all believers make up the body of Christ and that each of us has received at least one spiritual gift. Many of us have received two or more.

There are a number of passages in the New Testament that refer to spiritual gifts, but I would like to focus on two in particular: Romans 12:6–8 and Ephesians 4:11. These two portions of Scripture provide a representative list of some of the major spiritual gifts. In Romans 12:6–8, we see the gifts of prophecy, service, teaching, exhortation, giving, leadership, and showing mercy. Ephesians 4:11 lists apostleship, prophecy, evangelism, and pastor-teacher. Some of these spiritual gifts are discussed below.

The gift of *pastor-teacher* is a very special gift and one that comes with a very special calling from the Holy Spirit. The main characteristic of this gift is faithfulness to the calling to preach and to teach the Word of God. Another characteristic of this gift is that those called to this office should be a positive role model for their flock. Other traits include a loving and caring spirit and being able to handle criticism.

Another very special spiritual gift is that of *evangelism.* All believers are called to be witnesses to the world of the Good News of the gospel, but a certain group are called and gifted to be evangelists. Characteristic of this spiritual gift is a burning desire to reach the lost of this world by communicating the gospel in a simple and compelling way. This gift can be employed to reach large groups or may be exercised in small groups or individual settings.

Two other gifts, *teaching* and *exhortation,* have similar, yet distinctive, roles within the body. Teaching is the ability to communicate spiritually sound information in a simple and clear method, driven by love for the body of Christ and the Word of God. Exhortation is the ability to explain the Word of God and to translate it in a convincing way that makes it relevant in practical issues of life.

The last group of gifts can be loosely grouped together under the label of "serving gifts." They are *leadership, giving, service,* and *mercy.* Leadership is marked by an ability to show the way with biblical wisdom and to develop teams. The gift of giving is demonstrated in a person with the ability to accumulate and earn money so that he or she can give abundantly to the body. The gift of service is a special gift of sacrificial love and devotion in serving others, with a willingness to function behind the scenes. The gift of mercy allows the believer to recognize who is in pain or who is downtrodden and to comfort them.

We can see why spiritual gifts are so important to the church and in the lives of believers. Every believer needs to know and practice his or her spiritual gift for the building up of the kingdom of God.

ACTION STEP:

Read and review what the Bible says about spiritual gifts in 1 Corinthians 12. Seek out your spiritual gift. Ask God to show you your area of giftedness and how you might use this gift in the building up of the body of Christ.

FOR FURTHER READING:

He Gave Gifts
pp. 1–44
Charles R. Swindoll

Section 7

A DISCIPLINED LIFE

40
What We Hear

So I strive always to keep my conscience clear before God and man (Acts 24:16 NIV*).*

One of the topics I addressed in the first volume of *Basics for Believers* was discipline. I gave the reader a definition of discipline and a brief review of its importance in every area of our lives.

Discipline affects everything we do, and without it we will suffer very serious consequences, especially in the spiritual realm. For this reason, starting with this chapter, I will address six aspects of life that are common to all people and frequently serve as the portals of entry that determine who we become, how we behave, what we believe, and, ultimately, what we are. These things are what we *hear,* what we *see,* what we *read,* what we *say,* what we *think,* and what we *do.*

Recognizing how important it is to guard these practices is at the heart of what it is to be a believer in the Lord Jesus Christ. Most of what eventually becomes failure and defeat in the life of Christians can be traced to its point of entry in one of these activities.

There is a story that provides an excellent analogy of the priority of this guardianship. As the story goes, there was a village that employed a "keeper of the spring." The spring was the source of the village's water supply. As time passed, the villagers forgot why they needed the man—namely, to keep the spring clean of debris—so they dismissed him. Soon their water became polluted. They spent a great deal of time and effort to solve the problem, but with poor results. Finally, someone remembered that they had had a keeper of the spring whose job it was to prevent debris from collecting in the waters, thus guaranteeing a flow of uncontaminated water to the village.

How we believers need our own "keeper of the springs" today! Our culture is awash in the most abhorrent forms of pollution, and they invade our lives at every level.

Let's begin with that wonderful gift of hearing. Imagine not being able to hear music or laughter or the sound of great expressions of oratory. What a wonderful gift from God is hearing! Yet without applying guardianship over what we hear, we can easily allow pollution to penetrate our person.

There are so many sources of "sound pollution" today. Many of the music lyrics promoted and played on today's radio and presented on CDs and in concerts represent a man-centered focus and romanticism that encourages adultery, fornication, lust, envy, pride, covetousness, violence, and baseness. With this kind of influence, it is no wonder that our culture has become so tolerant and "open-minded" toward evil and shameful behavior.

Another area of pollution that has ridden the rails of sound into our minds is the off-color, racial, sexual, and lewd humor of our times. Much of society—many believers included—has become too tolerant of this type of communication. Most makers of today's movies seem preoccupied with using as much foul language as possible. Just think how far we have come since the great debate of the late 1930s, when the use of one curse word in the three-hour movie *Gone with the Wind* created such a stir.

As believers we need to guard what we allow to enter our minds through what we hear. We need to avoid the pollution that travels over the airways and into our hearts and minds.

ACTION STEP:

List the things you hear that do not serve you well, including the movies and television you watch, the music you listen to, and the conversation you engage in. Using this list, think about how you can avoid exposing yourself to these influences.

FOR FURTHER READING:

The Glorious Pursuit
chapter 7, pp. 75–84
Gary L. Thomas

41
What We See

And if your eye causes you to sin, gouge it out. It is better to enter the Kingdom of God half blind than to have two eyes and be thrown into hell (Mark 9:47).

Most people would likely say that sight is one of the most precious gifts our Creator has given us.

I can remember even at an early age enjoying so much of the beauty God has created. I enjoyed—and still enjoy—colorful pictures and paintings, the stunning burst of fireworks, and the panorama of colors at the circus. Then there are the bright hues of the changing seasons, the brilliance of sunrises and sunsets, and the magnificence of the mountains and the seashore. And what can be more delightful than the beauty of a smile on the face of a loved one? What can evoke the emotions that come from gazing at a newborn baby, or summon the wonder that comes from examining the intricacies of a flower? The world is full of God's beauty, and it is an extraordinary privilege to be able to visually absorb these things.

The Bible reminds us that the heavens declare the glory of God and that the world around us demonstrates His handiwork. So much around us is breathtakingly beautiful and marvelous in its makeup.

On the other hand, the Bible also has much to say about the potential danger that confronts our eyes and about the need for every believer to be guarded in this area. Psalm 119:37 warns us against being caught up with worthless or meaningless things in this life. I can't think of a better recipient of this warning than the millions of people who fill their eyes every day with the "worthless things" presented on their television sets.

The Bible warns us against the potential to be provoked into lustful desires. In Job 31:1, Job says, "I made a covenant with my eyes not to look with lust upon a young woman." In the gospel of Mark, Jesus warned us not to allow the weakness of one part of our bodies to affect our hearts and lead us to sin (9:42–50).

The seeds of sin start with the temptation that enters our minds through our eyes. If we are going to live a victorious life in Christ, we must guard what we allow our eyes to dwell on. No one today can completely avoid images such as suggestive sexual ads or images that may be outright pornography, but we need to avoid these visual temptations as much as possible.

We must use reminders from God's Word to help us stay our course in this area. We need to realize that temptation is all around us. Even a man after God's own heart, King David, sinned when he was tempted by something he saw. All believers need to guard what they expose themselves to, especially if they tend to be visually oriented. Believers should avoid movies and television that contain visual nudity or suggestive behavior or that dishonor the Persons of the Godhead.

It has been said that the best defense is a good offense, and that applies in this area. As believers, we need to be proactive in seeking out alternatives to help us guard against visual temptation. If we have developed bad habits in regard to what we allow ourselves to view, the first step is to confess the habit as sin and seek God's forgiveness and ask Him for the strength to change. Changing the way you approach what you look at will be a huge step toward taking control of what enters your mind.

ACTION STEP:

Make a list of situations where you can be exposed to images you know are not good for you to see. Think about how you might avoid those situations and about positive substitutes for the negative images you will be avoiding.

FOR FURTHER READING:

When Good Men Are Tempted
pp. 121–34
Bill Perkins

42

What We Read

Do not be conformed to this world but be transformed by the renewal of your mind, that you may prove what is the will of God, what is good and acceptable and perfect (Romans 12:2 RSV).

In "A Disciplined Life," section 7 of the first volume of *Basics for Believers*, I stressed the vital role reading plays in the life of a believer. When we are young, reading is vital in the development of our understanding and in the gaining of information. As we mature, the ability to read continues to play a dominant role in most areas of the believer's life, especially in the spiritual. However, there is another side of reading that I want to address in this section.

We live in a marvelous age of availability and range when it comes to reading materials. We have a never-ending array of books, magazines, newspapers, and information systems on the Web, as well as an avalanche of flyers and pamphlets. The quality and readability of most printed materials today is outstanding, and the packaging and graphic presentation invite the reader to become engaged.

For the believer, there is an incredible abundance of materials in the spiritual area. The availability and accessibility to such materials is staggering. Unfortunately, though, a great deal of this data is not accurate or helpful in our walk with Christ, and much of it is potentially dangerous. What we choose to read is much like what we choose to listen to or look at, in that these choices come with lasting consequences. How do we make wise decisions in this area?

The first and foremost desire of every child of God should be to read God's Word, the Bible. If you are not starting at this foundational point, not only are you missing God's plan for your life, but you will be unable to determine what His plan and will actually are. Without the Bible's influence, you will fall prey to destructive influences and lead a defeated life.

In His infinite wisdom, God understood and anticipated our needs before He created anything. At the appropriate time, God, using various authors inspired by His Holy Spirit, wrote the Bible. As believers, we can be confident that God has provided in that book everything we need to lead a life that is pleasing to Him.

In Romans 12:2, the apostle Paul makes a plea to all believers *not* to copy the behavior of the world but to allow God to transform them by changing the way they think. One of the ways God changes the way we think is by teaching us through His Word.

Here are some simple guidelines for you to use in selecting and investing time in reading:

1. Begin every day by first reading God's Word.
2. Use a good study Bible to help you with references as you read.
3. Secure a good systematic theology to read.
4. Begin to read good commentaries on specific books of the Bible.
5. Read good books on specific topics you are drawn to as you read the Bible.

As you follow these guidelines, you will be successful in allowing God to transform your mind through His written Word.

ACTION STEP:

Make a commitment to read from the Bible every day for one month. This reading can be short or long, but remember to stay faithful to your commitment. In a journal or notepad write out the things you observe as you read and note how they may apply to your own walk with God.

FOR FURTHER READING:

The Pillars of Christian Character
chapter 6, pp. 67–81
John F. MacArthur

43
What We Say

We all make many mistakes, but those who control their tongues can also control themselves in every other way (James 3:2).

A couple of years ago, I heard something that made a lasting impression on me and reminds me to this day of what our culture has come to as it relates to how we talk. I was enjoying a cup of coffee at a local McDonald's restaurant in my hometown one Saturday morning when I overheard a conversation between two junior high school girls who were sitting in a nearby booth. I could not believe the language these young girls were using. I was startled at how such crude and vulgar expressions could come out of such young mouths. Their talk was filled with words that in the past would have been heard only in very bad environments and only from hardened adults.

Joseph Stowell, the president of Moody Bible Institute, has written an excellent book titled *The Weight of Your Words*. In this book, Stowell gives a clear definition of what the Bible says about the power of the tongue and the impact—positive or negative—words can have. He cites what the book of James has to say about the effect of words on marriages, families, our working environment, our friendships, and society overall. Stowell makes the key point that it is impossible to completely control our tongues unless we have supernatural strength from the person of the Holy Spirit.

James 3 points out five principles concerning the gravity of our words. First, we are not spiritually mature if we cannot control our tongues. Second, even though the tongue is small, it has the capacity to do great damage. Third, words are potentially combustible; they have the capacity to destroy. Fourth, if we do not submit our speech to the power of the Holy Spirit, our tongue will be like a deadly beast. Fifth, we have the ability to speak in conflicting manners with the same tongue.

Looking at these five principles, it should be clear how much evil is possible in the uncontrolled tongue. All believers need to pray that the Holy Spirit will help them discipline their tongues and work toward gaining the spiritual maturity that comes from learning to rule this powerful instrument. Not only do we need to endeavor to master our speech, but we need to be proactive in applying what the Bible says about how we transform our minds and how this transformation affects every part of our being, including what we say.

ACTION STEP:

Make a list of situations where you need to bring your tongue under control. Ask God to transform your heart and mind through His Spirit, which is the first step in controlling your tongue.

FOR FURTHER READING:

The Weight of Your Words: Measuring the Impact of What You Say
Joseph M. Stowell

44

What We Think

The LORD doesn't make decisions the way you do! People judge by outward appearance, but the LORD looks at a person's thoughts and intentions (1 Samuel 16:7).

For the past eighteen years, I have spent the majority of my professional career in the Christian book publishing industry and have been involved with the Christian Booksellers Association (CBA). In 1999, this organization came up with a new slogan that captured what the industry is all about. The slogan reads, "What goes into the mind comes out in a life."

This is an appropriate motto for our industry, as it is a clear reminder of the scriptural truth that most believers overlook far too often: Sin begins in the mind! The Bible exhorts us to guard our hearts—the center of our consciousness—and to keep our minds focused on the truth.

Several years ago, in the book *The Battle for the Mind,* Tim LaHaye stressed the power of the mind and the disastrous effect man's wisdom, through the religion of humanism, has had on it. He wrote, "Most scientists agree that although we cannot consciously control all the functions of our brain, most people could regulate far more of them than they realize. One thing is certain: What you see, what you hear, and the way you think [your philosophy of life] are the most significant influences on your life."

Far too many believers naively believe that they can allow themselves to think nonbiblically and not suffer negative consequences. Believers who are poorly grounded in the truth of the Scriptures don't have a reference point from which to make wise decisions when it comes to what they think about. Many assume that they are doing fine just so long as they are not preoccupied with clearly sinful thoughts. Yet, in many cases those subjects that consume a vast majority of our time can be the very things that keep us from dwelling on eternal matters.

So many of us are so driven, so wired and connected, and have so much to do that we never get to the only things that ultimately matter: our relationship with God, service for Him, and intimacy with the Savior. Our minds are continually bombarded by facts, situations, and circumstances to the point that we don't have time to think and meditate on the things of God as revealed in His Word.

The challenge for every believer is to keep the main thing the main thing. We are to use our minds to grow in the knowledge of and service to our Lord, to build His kingdom by reaching out to a lost world, and to love our neighbors as we love ourselves. As we become obedient to these great commandments, God in His wondrous grace pours out His blessings upon us.

Admittedly, this practice is not easy to develop. We all struggle our sinful natures. We all live in a world full of distractions and enticements, and we all battle against evil forces. Yet it is possible to have victory in how we use our minds—what we allow to go into them and what we keep as our main focus. This is possible only if we allow the Holy Spirit to work in our lives. It also requires discipline on our part.

We need to be proactive in this area, especially in the spiritual realm. The best way to keep our minds focused on the things of God is to read His Word, talk to Him continually, and think about how awesome and wonderful He is. Focus on His unfailing mercies, grace, and love. As the Bible commands us, "Think on these things" (Philippians 4:8 KJV).

ACTION STEP:

Take one average day in your life and journal everything you think about. Ask yourself how your thoughts align with the truth of God's Word. Then think of ways to keep your thoughts centered on God.

FOR FURTHER READING:

Loving God with All Your Mind
chapters 1 and 2, pp. 11–46
Elizabeth George

45

What We Do

Dear brothers and sisters, what's the use of saying you have faith if you don't prove it by your actions? That kind of faith can't save anyone (James 2:14).

There is a well-known statement that summarizes the Bible's definition of true saving faith: "What you do is what you believe!" Think about this statement for a moment and then relate it to where you can see the church is headed today.

George Barna, who has done extensive research on the Christian church, stated in one of his recent books that, in many areas, professing Christians differ from unbelievers very little in how they live. This is a sad statement, but I believe it is a true one. If we take a look at the divorce rate, the number of lawsuits, service to the community, and caring for the poor within the church, there is little that distinguishes believers from the rest of the world.

When you consider the things we allow to influence us, it should come as no surprise that a vast number of Christians are weak and ineffectual in living out their faith in this world and, consequently, have little or no impact for the cause of Christ.

Many believers have slowly drifted away from their first love, Jesus Christ, and have lost sight of the Cross and the sacrifice God made for them. They have lost touch with the power of the indwelling Holy Spirit and have forgotten the truths of the awesome, sovereign God of the Bible.

Because they feed upon the junk of this world, many believers have lost the time and appetite for the things of God. Trivial pursuits so preoccupy the minds of many of God's people that they have lost sight of what's really important. Most believers admire the Bible, but they seldom read it. They pray only on those occasions when their minds are stirred. Sadly, few believers ever experience God's wondrous power, which is displayed through the devotion and dedication of a consistent, serious, and focused prayer life.

But the most noticeable area of similarity between those in the church and those on the outside is the worship of self. We live in a culture and a time when the vast majority of decisions are made based not on truth, integrity, or consideration for others, but on what is best for *me* or what will bring *me* pleasure and serve *my* best interests. Sadly, this way of thinking is all too common in the church. But it is not the way God has instructed us to be.

In the Old Testament book of Hosea, we can read about how God's love is characterized. This is the standard we are to strive for. When we believers begin to grasp just how unlovable and unlovely we are, a transformation in our attitude toward others becomes possible. And if we truly are believers, we will work to change our actions.

True believers are called to deny self, to endure injustice, persecution, unfair treatment, and all forms of adversity that those of the world will not tolerate.

It is not what you *profess* to believe that matters, but what you *do*—day in and day out, when things are good or bad, when things are fair or unfair, and when others see us or no one but God is looking.

ACTION STEP:

Honestly answer these questions: How regularly do you read the Bible? How often do you spend time in prayer? When was the last time you put aside your rights for the glory of God's name? How often do you get alone with God? Finally, ask yourself how you are different from those who don't know Jesus Christ.

FOR FURTHER READING:

Our Covenant God
chapter 13, pp. 128–34
Kay Arthur

46
What We Are

Keep your heart with all diligence, for out of it spring the issues of life (Proverbs 4:23 NKJV).

Someone once said that what you really are is the way you are when no one else is around. There is a lot of truth in this statement.

We live in a world that has gone image crazy and where the right spin on something is more important than the actual truth of the matter. Character and integrity are of small consequence—it's perception that counts. Our world worships famous personalities, fabulous programs, and fantastic products. But if we should come to discover the entire truth about these things, we would likely find deception and lies. We live in an age when clever people can take facts and twist them to such an extent that justice is mocked. Obvious evil is called good, and blatant sin is debated on the basis of semantics.

Unfortunately, most believers have been exposed to or influenced by this aspect of the world's thinking. So it is critical that we take a hard look at ourselves to see if this kind of thinking and behavior has become a part of who we are. The Bible has a lot to say about deception, including self-deception, and we are well served to examine some key points regarding "what we are."

The Gospels tell us that Jesus confronted the phony spiritual trappings of the Pharisees. Because He was God, He knew their hearts and their selfish motives. He knew of their emphasis on image and perception.

Paul warns of the dangers of the last days, in which we are now living, when people will consider nothing sacred, will be unloving and unforgiving, and will have no interest in what is good—all the while holding to a form of religiosity. The apostle warns that evil people and impostors will flourish and work at deceiving others as they themselves have been deceived. Paul added that many will be consumed with a love of money and self.

The Bible encourages those who profess to be disciples of Jesus Christ to examine themselves and look not only at what they do but at their motives for doing it. As followers of Christ, we are called to make our election and calling certain. We are to examine ourselves against the only standard that matters: the truth of the Word of God.

In the gospel of Matthew, our Lord uttered some sobering and frightening words on this subject. "Not everyone who says to Me, 'Lord, Lord,' shall enter the kingdom of heaven, but he who does the will of My Father in heaven. Many will say to Me in that day, 'Lord, Lord, have we not prophesied in Your name, cast out demons in Your name, and done many wonders in Your name?' And then I will declare to them, 'I never knew you, depart from Me, you who practice lawlessness!'" (Matthew 7:21–23 NKJV).

Ultimately, all that will matter in eternity is the answer to this question: Do you truly know God, and does He know you? What we are, how we live, and the motives of our hearts reveal the answer to this question.

ACTION STEP:

Examine what you are by taking an honest look at how you live and your motivations for what you do. What do these things tell you about your relationship with God?

FOR FURTHER READING:

Keeping the Heart
John Flavel

Section 8

A GOAL-ORIENTED LIFE

47

Heroes

And what more shall I say? I do not have time to tell about Gideon, Barak, Samson, Jephthah, David, Samuel and the prophets, who through faith conquered kingdoms, administered justice, and gained what was promised; who shut the mouths of lions, quenched the fury of flames, and escaped the edge of the sword; whose weakness was turned to strength; and who became powerful in battle and routed foreign armies (Hebrews 11:32–34 NIV).

Some time ago, as I was on my commute home at the end of the day, I encountered a major traffic jam in front of the restaurant Planet Hollywood. At first, I thought there had been an accident, but I soon recognized that the commotion was caused by what appeared to be thousands of young people converging at the entryway of the restaurant.

As I made my way through this mass of people, cars, and police on horseback, I finally saw the object of everyone's attention—the members of a rock band. As they stepped out of the building and made their way to a waiting bus, screams rang out from the crowd and there was a rush by those trying to get as close as possible to the musicians. The members of this band were heroes, idols who had captivated the hearts of that crowd.

This is not an unusual picture. In fact, it is played out regularly around the world as people show their love and devotion to the musicians, actors, athletes, politicians, and other celebrities who are their heroes. I think it reveals a lot about our culture today when we examine the individuals or groups we make our heroes.

The Bible has something to say about heroes. The writer of Hebrews 11, which has been called "The Saints' Hall of Fame" and "The Heroes of Faith" chapter, records a long list of people whose faith made them more than conquerors. Every one of these individuals had one thing in common: They lived by faith in almighty God. Each of them displayed weakness, and some had failed greatly, but all were faithful to the purposes to which God had called them. History is full of other great heroes of the Christian faith who have demonstrated how God is pleased to use saved sinners to help build His kingdom.

God has continued to raise up heroes—those whose examples we can follow and who have lived a wonderful life of faith in the risen Lord. One of my favorite heroes of the faith is Dwight Lyman Moody, the founder of the educational institution I work for, Moody Bible Institute. Moody also founded the publishing division of which I am a part, Moody Press.

D. L. Moody has influenced my life in many ways. The more I learn about this man, the more I can see how the Lord developed his natural gifts so that he became a great channel to be used of Him. Moody exemplified commitment to the life's mission God had given Him. Because of this commitment, Moody was not afraid to take risks when he sensed God's leading, and he grew to become a man of great vision.

There is little doubt that D. L. Moody could have been extremely successful in the business world, but instead he devoted his life to serving Christ. He strove to live a life directed by the Holy Spirit and one that reached out to others, particularly young people. Moody also had a teachable spirit. His whole life demonstrated that he was a learner. He was a humble man, and yet he moved easily among every class of people.

What I admire and love most about D. L. Moody was his love for souls. He had a true passion for allowing God to use him to win people to Christ. Moody continues to impact those who are familiar with his life.

If you need a true hero, check out D. L. Moody, Billy Graham, Eric Liddell, Hudson Taylor, Lottie Moon, or Amy Carmichael—to name a few. These are the heroes whose legacies will never die, for their lives demonstrate the power of God to those whose wills are surrendered to His calling.

ACTION STEP:

Read about the heroes I have mentioned above. Then write down the character traits and the actions that made them heroes of the faith. In what ways would you like to emulate these people?

FOR FURTHER READING:

A Passion for Souls: The Life of D. L. Moody
chapter 13, pp. 387–412
Lyle W. Dorsett

48

Mentoring

You have heard me teach many things that have been confirmed by many reliable witnesses. Teach these great truths to trustworthy people who are able to pass them on to others (2 Timothy 2:2).

In one of the most recent, and many say the best, biographies of the famous evangelist D. L. Moody, author Lyle Dorsett, in his book *A Passion for Souls*, summarizes what he felt were the ten key characteristics that produced the extraordinary effectiveness that marked Moody's life and ministry. Number seven of that list is "A Confidence in Young People."

Moody started his ministry with the disadvantaged youngsters on the streets of Chicago. As his ministry grew, his life continued to display the great value he placed on the mentoring of young people. One of the reasons Moody knew the importance of investing in others, especially in the young, was that he knew how frequently the subject is addressed in the Bible.

As believers, we are commanded and encouraged to pass along our faith and the foundational principles of living to the young people around us. Sadly, this is another one of those traditions being lost in today's culture. Much of today's youth population is being raised by TV, videos, and motion pictures and the false characters they portray.

Other youths learn the principles of life on the streets through gangs. It is reported that one of the main reasons for the growth of gangs is the absence of father figures or leaders in the lives of these youngsters. This critical time of growing up, which occurs between the ages of six to sixteen, has been left void, and young people often have no one to teach them how to live.

If we are going to impact the world for Christ and His kingdom, then every believer needs to become involved in this area. There are millions of young people who desperately need someone to mentor them, giving them time and attention and demonstrating to them the true characteristics of love. These children need good role models after whom they can pattern their lives. They need real heroes who are open and honest, who will guide them in the way of truth, who will show them the way to lasting peace and happiness.

At this point, many might say, "OK, but I don't know the first thing about mentoring or if I am someone who can even do it." If that is the case with you, I recommend that you read the book *As Iron Sharpens Iron—Building Character in a Mentoring Relationship* by Howard and William Hendricks. It is an excellent manual for those seeking to be mentored and for those willing to become mentors. It is a practical A-to-Z book written to serve as a manual on this subject.

We all need to remember that it is through children that the future is being established, for good or for bad.

ACTION STEP:

Make up your mind to do three things in the coming year: (1) Get involved with a young person who needs mentoring; (2) locate and support a youth ministry; and (3) share their needs in this area with other adults.

FOR FURTHER READING:

As Iron Sharpens Iron—BuildingCharacter in a Mentoring Relationship
Howard and William Hendricks

49
Reproducing

Live wisely among those who are not Christians, and make the most of every opportunity. Let your conversation be gracious and effective so that you will have the right answer for everyone (Colossians 4:5–6).

One of the chapters in the first volume of *Basics for Believers* was titled "Reading." There I stated that "the apostle Paul knew the value of reading. He recognized that reading was a primary gateway to knowledge." The need to read widely is foundational to building our faith.

When a reader discovers an outstanding book on a specific topic, that person becomes enthused about it and recommends it to others. One such book I have read is on the subject of "reproducing believers" and is titled *Finding Common Ground—How to Communicate with Those Outside the Christian Community . . . While We Still Can.* In this book, author Tim Downs draws a clear distinction between two key elements in communicating to the world of nonbelievers. The first is what he calls *harvesting,* which we would recognize as evangelism, or the practice of sharing the gospel message. The second element he calls *sowing,* which is the preparation that gradually and naturally takes place in a way that opens the opportunity to present the gospel message to the readied heart.

We now live in a culture—the postmodern world where the worldview of most people has drastically changed from that of thirty years ago—that is not, for the most part, interested in the message of the gospel. If we are serious about fulfilling our Lord's commandment to be involved in the activity of spiritually reproducing, we need to be certain we are solidly grounded in the Scriptures and are knowledgeable about the basics of our faith. We also need to understand the things taking place around us in order to intelligently interact with those outside the evangelical subculture.

Along with these first two points, we need to reevaluate our understanding of the concept of sowing and why this spiritual discipline is so critically needed today. We must recognize the balance between the requirements of love, which engages a person where their needs are, and those of justice, which God requires.

Another important area of sowing we need to stress is that of including both "science" and "art" in all of our communications. The term *science* refers to the substance or core thought of the message. *Art* refers to the style and flow of the presentation of the message—the way we communicate the message through our words and phrases.

It is unfortunate that much of the Christian message focuses so much on the "science" of the message while neglecting the "art" side. This is especially true today in an age where there is such an emphasis on communication. If believers do not develop the skills required to deliver an effective message from an "art" perspective, then the wonderful message of hope will have no impact.

If you doubt this point, take a look at the Bible, God's library for life. We know the Word is absolute "science," or truth and substance. But look at how it is written. Much of it is beautiful in its "art." Jesus' parables are examples of this. They are powerful messages of truth wrapped in examples of life that have made an impact for centuries.

Believers need to grow in their knowledge of the Scriptures and theology and in their ability to be persuasive and appealing in the way they deliver the truth, so that the sinner's heart will be ready for the convicting work of the Holy Spirit.

ACTION STEP:

Take time to evaluate yourself on your ability to articulate both the "science" as well as the "art" of the gospel message. Use the Lord's parables to enable you to develop both of these elements of effective witnessing.

FOR FURTHER READING:

Finding Common Ground—How to Communicate with Those Outside the Christian Community . . . While We Still Can
Introduction through chapter 2, pp. 11–32
Tim Downs

50
Trustworthiness

At this, the administrators and the satraps tried to find grounds for charges against Daniel in his conduct of government affairs, but they were unable to do so. They could find no corruption in him, because he was trustworthy and neither corrupt nor negligent (Daniel 6:4 NIV*).*

I have written much of this book to give believers greater knowledge of the foundational truths from the Bible. Other sections of this book deal with the impact these truths have on believers when the power of the Holy Spirit quickens our minds to their reality.

True believers are in the process of being changed from the old life to the new, and nowhere should this be more evident than in the area of trustworthiness. Believers should be people who tell the truth, live by the truth, and forsake anything that brings into question their testimony of being trustworthy.

As is true in nearly every facet of the Christian life, it is easy to allow our trustworthiness to become compromised. When this happens, our relationship with our Lord suffers, as does our testimony to those around us.

The believer's testimony can be powerful in this regard because the consistent quality of trustworthiness is becoming rare in our society today. Let me give you a few examples: It was reported that in 1997 retailers lost in excess of $9 billion to shoplifting and another $10 billion due to theft by their own employees. In the area of our personal income taxes, it is estimated that a significant number of Americans are not completely honest in their yearly filing of tax returns.

Another clear demonstration of the lack of trustworthiness prevalent in our age is the amount of bad debt that must be written off every year. It is also easy for consumers to be taken advantage of through false advertising or misleading sales or specials. Deceptive practices are increasingly becoming the norm for all segments of business today.

The most disturbing aspect of this revelation is that these practices are not limited to nonbelievers. Many believers operate within the same guidelines as the world. That causes lost blessings from God, lost witness to unbelievers around us, and lost fellowship with our Lord.

Even the "little" offenses in this area weaken the spiritual life of a believer and keep him or her from the joy that comes from being trustworthy. All believers will be tempted in this area of integrity, and some will tell "little white lies," not realizing that any lie is a sin. As employees, some believers are not completely trustworthy in their responsibilities in the workplace. Still others are deceptive and outright dishonest as they manipulate facts for their own gain.

It is clear in the Scriptures that revival always starts in the hearts of believers. Recently I was inspired by the witness of a believer who was very successful in his business. He told me that he had made a commitment to operate his company on the basis of being current in all of his payments to his vendors, even though it is standard procedure to take extra time for payment.

That is making trustworthiness a priority. In the long run God will bless this in ways that will astonish everyone.

God wants us to be trustworthy in every area of our lives—period. We need to examine how we conduct ourselves in this area and make sure that we please God by being trustworthy believers.

ACTION STEP:

Take an inventory of your trustworthiness and make a note of anything you may need to change. Confess it as sin and ask God to help you be trustworthy in every area of your life.

FOR FURTHER READING:

The Life You've Always Wanted:
Spiritual Disciplines for the Ordinary Person
chapter 11, pp. 189–204
John Ortberg

51
Character

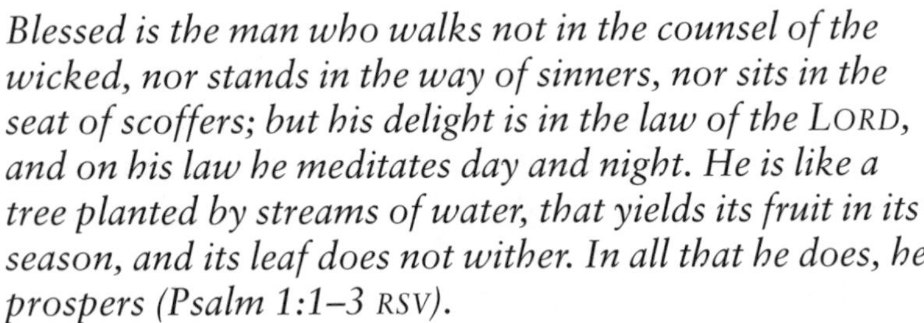
Blessed is the man who walks not in the counsel of the wicked, nor stands in the way of sinners, nor sits in the seat of scoffers; but his delight is in the law of the L*ORD*, *and on his law he meditates day and night. He is like a tree planted by streams of water, that yields its fruit in its season, and its leaf does not wither. In all that he does, he prospers (Psalm 1:1–3* RSV*).*

There is a type of pine tree that grows in some sections of the southern United States that can reach sixty feet or more in height. These trees have sizable trunks and appear to be strongly planted in the ground, but, as most people who have been around them for very long recognize, they can be very vulnerable to storms. They have a limited root structure and can easily fall in strong winds.

A stark contrast to this pine is the oak tree, which develops an extraordinary root system as it grows. Mature oak trees can endure violent winds and remain firmly planted in the ground. It is almost unheard of for a healthy oak to be blown over by wind.

These two trees are excellent analogies to the contrast between the person who only *appears* to have solid character and the one who truly *is* strong in character. Both of these people may appear to be strong, but only the one who is deeply rooted in the things of God has true character.

Character is an attribute that is developed over a long period of time, beginning with influences from our childhood. Parents have a profound impact on the character development of their children. The true character of the parents will, with few exceptions, show up in their children.

Character is what determines the conduct of a person, especially in times of trial, stress, or temptation. It is during the hard times that character is tested the most and grows the most.

The depth of our relationship with God is the basis of our true character. This is an example of God's grace, in that God in His love provided for the development of character qualities—such as honesty, kindness, faithfulness, mercy, and humility—that can serve as blessings to those around us.

Although believers and nonbelievers alike can develop many of the character qualities I just listed, God has given the believer a much higher standard for godly character. We have been commanded to develop godly character, which demonstrates itself with distinctive qualities that are foreign to the natural man. For example, God commanded us not only to love our brothers and sisters and friends, but also our enemies. Jesus commanded that if our enemy is hungry, we should feed him, and if he is thirsty, we should give him drink. He also commanded us to pray for those who persecute us and care for those who abuse us and slander us. We are called to give to those who steal from us. We are never to avenge ourselves, but to leave vengeance to the Lord. We are not to return evil for evil. Our only debt to others is to love them, for this fulfills all the commandments.

Jesus set the example for us in the way He lived when He was on earth. We should never forget that Christ lived His life completely controlled by the Holy Spirit and fully surrendered to the will of His Father.

As we grow in godly character, we will become more and more like our Savior and Lord, Jesus Christ. When that happens, we will be lights that shine forth in darkness.

ACTION STEP:

Honestly examine your own character by thinking about how you respond to trials, stress, temptation, or wrongdoing by those around you. Ask yourself what you need to change in order to be more like Jesus Christ. Then ask God to empower you by His Spirit to make the changes you need to make.

FOR FURTHER READING:

Kingdom Life in a Fallen World
Sinclair B. Ferguson

52
Godliness

Since everything will be destroyed in this way, what kind of people ought you to be? You ought to live holy and godly lives as you look forward to the day of God and speed its coming (2 Peter 3:11–12 NIV*).*

The highest compliment any believer can receive is to be told that he or she is a truly godly person. All believers are godly on occasion, but few display godliness on a consistent basis. Yet this is what God desires for all of His children.

All of us have known Christians who have the gifts of preaching and teaching, service to the kingdom, or kindness and mercy. But even among those people, few live consistently godly lives. One of the central messages of the Bible is how to become a godly person. It is vital that we understand this subject well so that we can fulfill God's plan for our lives.

The first thing we need to know about godliness is what the word means. Godliness is the discipline of being consumed with a growing devotion to God. It involves keeping God at the center of every aspect of our lives. This attitude can best be understood by examining the different components of devotion to God, the first of which is our attitude of reverence for Him.

I would define the word *reverence* as "wondering awe, tinged with fear, inspired by the sublime." Notice that I started this definition with the word *wondering*. That is because I believe we should never stop being overwhelmed with a sense of wonder, coupled with reverence, for almighty God. Along with that wonder should be a fear (see chapter 27 of this book, "The Fear of God") that comes from an overpowering contemplation of the awesomeness of the persons of the Godhead.

Coupled with *awe* for God, we need to nurture *love* for God. We can do this by learning from the Scriptures who He is and what He has done to redeem for Himself His chosen people. We should continually offer Him praise and thanksgiving for the wonder of His amazing grace and for His continual mercies. We should always be careful to understand His love in the context of what was required at Calvary so that God could remain true to His holiness yet demonstrate His love by pouring out His wrath on His only Son.

As we combine awe for God with our desire to love Him more and more, we will grow in our hunger to pursue Him and to establish a growing relationship with Him. As these attitudes become increasingly a part of who we are, our desire to please Him will grow and we will enjoy greater peace and joy.

As we develop in the discipline of godliness, the Holy Spirit will confirm within our hearts that we are in the center of God's plan and purpose for our lives. We will, as the apostle Paul proclaimed in Philippians 3:12, "keep working toward that day when [we] will finally be all that Christ Jesus saved [us] for and wants [us] to be."

ACTION STEP:

Review the main points of this section as you:
1. Think about the awesomeness of God.
2. Think about the time you spend with God and how you show love for Him.
3. Think about how much you really pursue God.
Pray and ask God to help you in your pursuit of true godliness.

FOR FURTHER READING:

Life Essentials: A Guide for Spiritual Growth
William L. Thrasher, Jr., General Editor

Summary

In 1999, a heartbreaking tragedy occurred at Columbine High School, located in Littleton, Colorado, in the greater Denver area. What should have been some of the best of times for the Columbine students turned into a living nightmare. Two of their fellow students, bent on a well-planned course of death and destruction, took the lives of thirteen of their classmates and one of their teachers, as well as seriously wounding many others.

One of the victims, Cassie Bernall, gained national attention because of the interaction that took place between her and her killer moments before her death. As the young killer approached Cassie, he heard her crying, "Oh my God! Oh my God!" He asked Cassie if she believed in God, to which she replied, "Yes, I do." The killer asked "Why?" then shot Cassie to death.

This exchange gained worldwide notoriety, as did Cassie's story leading up to that horrible day. This young woman was clearly recognized as someone unashamed of her faith in God and His Son, Jesus Christ. But that was not the most important part of the story. What had transpired in Cassie Bernall's life over the previous couple of years is what will have an impact for eternity.

After her death, Cassie's parents told a national television audience that from the time she entered her teen years, Cassie was caught up in some of the same destructive pursuits and behavior that eventually destroyed the lives of the two young men who would one day become ruthless murderers. Cassie had chosen a path of disobedience, hatred, and self-destruction, and it appeared there was no hope for rescuing this young woman.

But Cassie's parents did not give up. They fought to rescue her from the demonic influences to which she had fallen captive. Ultimately, Cassie met a new friend at a church retreat—which was one of the few outside activities Cassie's parents allowed her to take part in—and one evening the two ended up on a mountain ridge where they beheld the wonder of God's heaven.

Cassie and her friend talked about the awesome God who created this great expanse of stars and determined that if He could do that, surely He could make an impact on their lives. It was at this moment that the real story occurred, for that night Cassie passed from death to eternal life as she was changed into a new creation in Christ.

Cassie is now with our Lord and will forever rejoice at that instant when she was born from above. I would recommend that you read the complete story in a book entitled *She Said Yes: The Unlikely Martyrdom of Cassie Bernall* (by Misty Bernall and Madeleine L'Engle, Plough Publishing, 1999). The tragedy of a life cut short is a constant reminder of how death can come unexpectedly and early and how important it is that we know the true condition of our souls.

Cassie's salvation came as a result of looking out at the heavens and accepting the truth of almighty God. That is also where I started when I began to write volume 1 of *Basics for Believers.*

I believe one of the reasons God chose to create the heavens was to give men and women a visual reminder of His awesomeness and to demonstrate that He is beyond comprehension. At the same time, God has chosen to reveal Himself and communicate even more clearly with us in the Bible. It is when we come to accept this fact that we are able to respond to God in the appropriate way.

We need to understand that the knowledge and acceptance of the truth of Christ that leads to salvation is a gift from God. It is also vital as we grow in our faith that we keep before ourselves who God is and who we are. If we are to grow as true disciples, we need continually to behold God in the pages of Scripture and to see ourselves against the truth of Scripture—the true spiritual plumb line.

It is helpful regularly to look around and see the wonder of what God has created, even considering the effects of sin on creation. Also, on occasion we should get away to a place where we can look into the heavens and marvel at the endless universe God has made for us, just to remind us of Himself. This will give us a renewed sense of dedication to and awe at the mighty God we serve.

I bring this book to a conclusion with the following

Scriptures, which I pray will stimulate our hearts with thoughts of the God who at the beginning of time made heaven and earth by speaking everything into being, and who will be at the end of time when He brings about final judgment and ushers in eternity.

> In the beginning God created the heavens and the earth (Genesis 1:1).
>
> The heavens tell of the glory of God. The skies display his marvelous craftsmanship. Day after day they continue to speak; night after night they make him known (Psalm 19:1–2).
>
> In the beginning the Word already existed. He was with God, and he was God. He was in the beginning with God. He created everything there is. Nothing exists that he didn't make (John 1:1–3).
>
> Long ago God spoke many times and in many ways to our ancestors through the prophets. But now in these final days, he has spoken to us through his Son. God promised everything to the Son as an inheritance, and through the Son he made the universe and everything in it (Hebrews 1:1–2).
>
> Then Jesus said, "Come to me, all of you who are weary and carry heavy burdens, and I will give you rest. Take my yoke upon you. Let me teach you, because I am humble and gentle, and you will find rest for your souls" (Matthew 11:28–29).

Appendix A
More Tools for the Journey

Good tools are essential if we are going to do a job well. For this reason I have provided references to a number of important tools that will help you in the process of becoming a mature believer.

1. A study Bible:
   - *The Expanded Ryrie Study Bible*
   - *The John MacArthur Study Bible*
   - *The NIV Study Bible*
   - *The Life Application Study Bible*

2. An exhaustive concordance:
   - *The New Strong's Exhaustive Concordance of the Bible*
   - *NIV Exhaustive Concordance*
   - *NAS Exhaustive Concordance*
   - *NLT Exhaustive Concordance*

3. An instruction book on how to study the Bible:
   - *Living by the Book*, Howard Hendricks and William Hendricks
   - *How to Study Your Bible*, Kay Arthur
   - *How to Read the Bible for All Its Worth*, Gordon D. Fee and Douglas Stuart

4. *The New Treasury of Scripture Knowledge*

5. A Bible Dictionary:
   - *The New Unger's Bible Dictionary*
   - *The New Bible Dictionary*

6. A book on systematic theology:
   - *Systematic Theology,* Wayne Grudem
   - *Basic Theology,* Charles C. Ryrie

7. *Life Essentials—A Guide for Spiritual Growth*
   - This product by Moody Press is a loose-leaf binder with helpful ways to organize your spiritual life. (See section at the end of this book for more information.)

Appendix B
Bible Reading Plan

JANUARY

	Morning	*Evening*		*Morning*	*Evening*
1.	GEN. 1, 2	MATT. 1	17.	GEN. 41	MATT. 13:1–32
2.	GEN. 3, 4, 5	MATT. 2	18.	GEN. 42, 43	MATT. 13:33–58
3.	GEN. 6, 7, 8	MATT. 3	19.	GEN. 44, 45	MATT. 14:1–21
4.	GEN. 9, 10, 11	MATT. 4	20.	GEN. 46, 47, 48	MATT. 14:22–36
5.	GEN. 12, 13, 14	MATT. 5:1–26	21.	GEN. 49, 50	MATT. 15:1–20
6.	GEN. 15, 16, 17	MATT. 5:27–48	22.	EX. 1, 2, 3	MATT. 15:21–39
7.	GEN. 18, 19	MATT. 6	23.	EX. 4, 5, 6	MATT. 16
8.	GEN. 20, 21, 22	MATT. 7	24.	EX. 7, 8	MATT. 17
9.	GEN. 23, 24	MATT. 8	25.	EX. 9, 10	MATT. 18:1–20
10.	GEN. 25, 26	MATT. 9:1–17	26.	EX. 11, 12	MATT. 18:21–35
11.	GEN. 27, 28	MATT. 9:18–38	27.	EX. 13, 14, 15	MATT. 19:1–15
12.	GEN. 29, 30	MATT. 10:1–23	28.	EX. 16, 17, 18	MATT. 19:16–30
13.	GEN. 31, 32	MATT. 10:24–42	29.	EX. 19, 20, 21	MATT. 20:1–16
14.	GEN. 33, 34, 35	MATT. 11	30.	EX. 22, 23, 24	MATT. 20:17–34
15.	GEN. 36, 37	MATT. 12:1–21	31.	EX. 25, 26	MATT. 21:1–22
16.	GEN. 38, 39, 40	MATT. 12:22–50			

FEBRUARY

	Morning	*Evening*		*Morning*	*Evening*
1.	EX. 27, 28	MATT. 21:23–46	16.	LEV. 22, 23	MARK 1:1–22
2.	EX. 29, 30	MATT. 22:1–22	17.	LEV. 24, 25	MARK 1:23–45
3.	EX. 31, 32, 33	MATT. 22:23–46	18.	LEV. 26, 27	MARK 2
4.	EX. 34, 35, 36	MATT. 23:1–22	19.	NUM. 1, 2	MARK 3:1–21
5.	EX. 37, 38	MATT. 23:23–39	20.	NUM. 3, 4	MARK 3:22–35
6.	EX. 39, 40	MATT. 24:1–22	21.	NUM. 5, 6	MARK 4:1–20
7.	LEV. 1, 2, 3	MATT. 24:23–51	22.	NUM. 7	MARK 4:21–41
8.	LEV. 4, 5, 6	MATT. 25:1–30	23.	NUM. 8, 9, 10	MARK 5:1–20
9.	LEV. 7, 8, 9	MATT. 25:31–46	24.	NUM. 11, 12, 13	MARK 5:21–43
10.	LEV. 10, 11, 12	MATT. 26:1–19	25.	NUM. 14, 15	MARK 6:1–32
11.	LEV. 13	MATT. 26:20–54	26.	NUM. 16, 17	MARK 6:33–56
12.	LEV. 14	MATT. 26:55–75	27.	NUM. 18, 19, 20	MARK 7:1–13
13.	LEV. 15, 16, 17	MATT. 27:1–31	28.	NUM. 21, 22	MARK 7:14–37
14.	LEV. 18, 19	MATT. 27:32–66	29.	NUM. 23, 24, 25	MARK 8:1–21
15.	LEV. 20, 21	MATT. 28			

Divide chapters for Feb. 29 and read them Feb. 28 and Mar.1 when February has only 28 days.

MARCH

	MORNING	EVENING		MORNING	EVENING
1.	NUM. 26, 27	MARK 8:22–38	17.	DEUT. 29, 30	MARK 16
2.	NUM. 28, 29	MARK 9:1–29	18.	DEUT. 31, 32	LUKE 1:1–23
3.	NUM. 30, 31	MARK 9:30–50	19.	DEUT. 33, 34	LUKE 1:24–56
4.	NUM. 32, 33	MARK 10:1–31	20.	JOSH. 1, 2, 3	LUKE 1:57–80
5.	NUM. 34, 35, 36	MARK 10:32–52	21.	JOSH. 4, 5, 6	LUKE 2:1–24
6.	DEUT. 1, 2	MARK 11:1–19	22.	JOSH. 7, 8	LUKE 2:25–52
7.	DEUT. 3, 4	MARK 11:20–33	23.	JOSH. 9, 10	LUKE 3
8.	DEUT. 5, 6, 7	MARK 12:1–27	24.	JOSH. 11, 12, 13	LUKE 4:1–32
9.	DEUT. 8, 9, 10	MARK 12:28–44	25.	JOSH. 14, 15	LUKE 4:33–44
10.	DEUT. 11, 12, 13	MARK 13:1–13	26.	JOSH. 16, 17, 18	LUKE 5:1–16
11.	DEUT. 14, 15, 16	MARK 13:14–37	27.	JOSH. 19, 20	LUKE 5:17–39
12.	DEUT. 17, 18, 19	MARK 14:1–25	28.	JOSH. 21, 22	LUKE 6:1–26
13.	DEUT. 20, 21, 22	MARK 14:26–50	29.	JOSH. 23, 24	LUKE 6:27–49
14.	DEUT. 23, 24, 25	MARK 14:51–72	30.	JUDG. 1, 2	LUKE 7:1–30
15.	DEUT. 26, 27	MARK 15:1–26	31.	JUDG. 3, 4, 5	LUKE 7:31–50
16.	DEUT. 28	MARK 15:27–47			

APRIL

	MORNING	EVENING		MORNING	EVENING
1.	JUDG. 6, 7	LUKE 8:1–21	16.	1 SAM. 19, 20, 21	LUKE 15:11–32
2.	JUDG. 8, 9	LUKE 8:22–56	17.	1 SAM. 22, 23, 24	LUKE 16:1–18
3.	JUDG. 10, 11	LUKE 9:1–36	18.	1 SAM. 25, 26	LUKE 16:19–31
4.	JUDG. 12, 13, 14	LUKE 9:37–62	19.	1 SAM. 27, 28, 29	LUKE 17:1–19
5.	JUDG. 15, 16, 17	LUKE 10:1–24	20.	1 SAM. 30, 31	LUKE 17:20–37
6.	JUDG. 18, 19	LUKE 10:25–42	21.	2 SAM. 1, 2, 3	LUKE 18:1–17
7.	JUDG. 20, 21	LUKE 11:1–28	22.	2 SAM. 4, 5, 6	LUKE 18:18–43
8.	RUTH	LUKE 11:29–54	23.	2 SAM. 7, 8, 9	LUKE 19:1–28
9.	1 SAM. 1, 2, 3	LUKE 12:1–34	24.	2 SAM. 10, 11, 12	LUKE 19:29–48
10.	1 SAM. 4, 5, 6	LUKE 12:35–59	25.	2 SAM. 13, 14	LUKE 20:1–26
11.	1 SAM. 7, 8, 9	LUKE 13:1–21	26.	2 SAM. 15, 16	LUKE 20:27–47
12.	1 SAM. 10, 11, 12	LUKE 13:22–35	27.	2 SAM. 17, 18	LUKE 21:1–19
13.	1 SAM. 13, 14	LUKE 14:1–24	28.	2 SAM. 19, 20	LUKE 21:20–38
14.	1 SAM. 15, 16	LUKE 14:25–35	29.	2 SAM. 21, 22	LUKE 22:1–30
15.	1 SAM. 17, 18	LUKE 15:1–10	30.	2 SAM. 23, 24	LUKE 22:31–53

MAY

	Morning	Evening		Morning	Evening
1.	1 KINGS 1, 2	LUKE 22:54–71	17.	2 KINGS 18, 19	JOHN 6:22–44
2.	1 KINGS 3, 4, 5	LUKE 23:1–26	18.	2 KINGS 20, 21, 22	JOHN 6:45–71
3.	1 KINGS 6, 7	LUKE 23:27–38	19.	2 KINGS 23, 24, 25	JOHN 7:1–31
4.	1 KINGS 8, 9	LUKE 23:39–56	20.	1 CHR. 1, 2	JOHN 7:32–53
5.	1 KINGS 10, 11	LUKE 24:1–35	21.	1 CHR. 3, 4, 5	JOHN 8:1–20
6.	1 KINGS 12, 13	LUKE 24:36–53	22.	1 CHR. 6, 7	JOHN 8:21–36
7.	1 KINGS 14, 15	JOHN 1:1–28	23.	1 CHR. 8, 9, 10	JOHN 8:37–59
8.	1 KINGS 16, 17, 18	JOHN 1:29–51	24.	1 CHR. 11, 12, 13	JOHN 9:1–23
9.	1 KINGS 19, 20	JOHN 2	25.	1 CHR. 14, 15, 16	JOHN 9:24–41
10.	1 KINGS 21, 22	JOHN 3:1–21	26.	1 CHR. 17, 18, 19	JOHN 10:1–21
11.	2 KINGS 1, 2, 3	JOHN 3:22–36	27.	1 CHR. 20, 21, 22	JOHN 10:22–42
12.	2 KINGS 4, 5	JOHN 4:1–30	28.	1 CHR. 23, 24, 25	JOHN 11:1–17
13.	2 KINGS 6, 7, 8	JOHN 4:31–54	29.	1 CHR. 26, 27	JOHN 11:18–46
14.	2 KINGS 9, 10, 11	JOHN 5:1–24	30.	1 CHR. 28, 29	JOHN 11:47–57
15.	2 KINGS 12, 13, 14	JOHN 5:25–47	31.	2 CHR. 1, 2, 3	JOHN 12:1–19
16.	2 KINGS 15, 16, 17	JOHN 6:1–21			

JUNE

	Morning	Evening		Morning	Evening
1.	2 CHR. 4, 5, 6	JOHN 12:20–50	16.	NEH. 1, 2, 3	ACTS 2:1–13
2.	2 CHR. 7, 8, 9	JOHN 13:1–17	17.	NEH. 4, 5, 6	ACTS 2:14–47
3.	2 CHR. 10, 11, 12	JOHN 13:18–38	18.	NEH. 7, 8	ACTS 3
4.	2 CHR. 13–16	JOHN 14	19.	NEH. 9, 10, 11	ACTS 4:1–22
5.	2 CHR. 17, 18, 19	JOHN 15	20.	NEH. 12, 13	ACTS 4:23–37
6.	2 CHR. 20, 21, 22	JOHN 16:1–15	21.	ESTHER 1, 2, 3	ACTS 5:1–16
7.	2 CHR. 23, 24, 25	JOHN 16:16–33	22.	ESTHER 4, 5, 6	ACTS 5:17–42
8.	2 CHR. 26, 27, 28	JOHN 17	23.	ESTHER 7–10	ACTS 6
9.	2 CHR. 29, 30, 31	JOHN 18:1–23	24.	JOB 1, 2, 3	ACTS 7:1–19
10.	2 CHR. 32, 33	JOHN 18:24–40	25.	JOB 4, 5, 6	ACTS 7:20–43
11.	2 CHR. 34, 35, 36	JOHN 19:1–22	26.	JOB 7, 8, 9	ACTS 7:44–60
12.	EZRA 1, 2	JOHN 19:23–42	27.	JOB 10, 11, 12	ACTS 8:1–25
13.	EZRA 3, 4, 5	JOHN 20	28.	JOB 13, 14, 15	ACTS 8:26–40
14.	EZRA 6, 7, 8	JOHN 21	29.	JOB 16, 17, 18	ACTS 9:1–22
15.	EZRA 9, 10	ACTS 1	30.	JOB 19, 20	ACTS 9:23–43

JULY

	MORNING	EVENING		MORNING	EVENING
1.	JOB 21, 22	ACTS 10:1–23	17.	PS. 22, 23, 24	ACTS 20:1–16
2.	JOB 23, 24, 25	ACTS 10:24–48	18.	PS. 25, 26, 27	ACTS 20:17–38
3.	JOB 26, 27, 28	ACTS 11	19.	PS. 28, 29, 30	ACTS 21:1–14
4.	JOB 29, 30	ACTS 12	20.	PS. 31, 32, 33	ACTS 21:15–40
5.	JOB 31, 32	ACTS 13:1–23	21.	PS. 34, 35	ACTS 22
6.	JOB 33, 34	ACTS 13:24–52	22.	PS. 36, 37	ACTS 23:1–11
7.	JOB 35, 36, 37	ACTS 14	23.	PS. 38, 39, 40	ACTS 23:12–35
8.	JOB 38, 39	ACTS 15:1–21	24.	PS. 41, 42, 43	ACTS 24
9.	JOB 40, 41, 42	ACTS 15:22–41	25.	PS. 44, 45, 46	ACTS 25
10.	PS. 1, 2, 3	ACTS 16:1–15	26.	PS. 47, 48, 49	ACTS 26
11.	PS. 4, 5, 6	ACTS 16:16–40	27.	PS. 50, 51, 52	ACTS 27:1–25
12.	PS. 7, 8, 9	ACTS 17:1–15	28.	PS. 53, 54, 55	ACTS 27:26–44
13.	PS. 10, 11, 12	ACTS 17:16–34	29.	PS. 56, 57, 58	ACTS 28:1–15
14.	PS. 13–16	ACTS 18	30.	PS. 59, 60, 61	ACTS 28:16–31
15.	PS. 17, 18	ACTS 19:1–20	31.	PS. 62, 63, 64	ROM. 1
16.	PS. 19, 20, 21	ACTS 19:21–41`			

AUGUST

	MORNING	EVENING		MORNING	EVENING
1.	PS. 65, 66, 67	ROM. 2	17.	PS. 107, 108	ROM. 15:21–33
2.	PS. 68, 69	ROM. 3	18.	PS. 109, 110, 111	ROM. 16
3.	PS. 70, 71, 72	ROM. 4	19.	PS. 112–115	1 COR. 1
4.	PS. 73, 74	ROM. 5	20.	PS. 116–118	1 COR. 2
5.	PS. 75, 76, 77	ROM. 6	21.	PS. 119:1–48	1 COR. 3
6.	PS. 78	ROM. 7	22.	PS. 119:49–104	1 COR. 4
7.	PS. 79, 80, 81	ROM. 8:1–18	23.	PS. 119:105–176	1 COR. 5
8.	PS. 82, 83, 84	ROM. 8:19–39	24.	PS. 120–123	1 COR. 6
9.	PS. 85, 86, 87	ROM. 9	25.	PS. 124–127	1 COR. 7:1–24
10.	PS. 88, 89	ROM. 10	26.	PS. 128–131	1 COR. 7:25–40
11.	PS. 90, 91, 92	ROM. 11:1–21	27.	PS. 132–135	1 COR. 8
12.	PS. 93, 94, 95	ROM. 11:22–36	28.	PS. 136–138	1 COR. 9
13.	PS. 96, 97, 98	ROM. 12	29.	PS. 139–141	1 COR. 10:1–13
14.	PS. 99–102	ROM. 13	30.	PS. 142–144	1 COR. 10:14–33
15.	PS. 103, 104	ROM. 14	31.	PS. 145–147	1 COR. 11:1–15
16.	PS. 105, 106	ROM. 15:1–20			

SEPTEMBER

	Morning	*Evening*		*Morning*	*Evening*
1.	PS. 148–150	1 COR. 11:16–34	16.	PROV. 30, 31	2 COR. 8
2.	PROV. 1, 2	1 COR. 12	17.	ECCLES. 1, 2, 3	2 COR. 9
3.	PROV. 3, 4	1 COR. 13	18.	ECCLES. 4, 5, 6	2 COR. 10
4.	PROV. 5, 6	1 COR. 14:1–20	19.	ECCLES. 7, 8, 9	2 COR. 11:1–15
5.	PROV. 7, 8	1 COR. 14:21–40	20.	ECCLES. 10, 11, 12	2 COR. 11:16–33
6.	PROV. 9, 10	1 COR. 15:1–32	21.	SONGS 1, 2, 3	2 COR. 12
7.	PROV. 11, 12	1 COR. 15:33–58	22.	SONGS 4, 5	2 COR. 13
8.	PROV. 13, 14	1 COR. 16	23.	SONGS 6, 7, 8	GAL. 1
9.	PROV. 15, 16	2 COR. 1	24.	ISAIAH 1, 2, 3	GAL. 2
10.	PROV. 17, 18	2 COR. 2	25.	ISAIAH 4, 5, 6	GAL. 3
11.	PROV. 19, 20	2 COR. 3	26.	ISAIAH 7, 8, 9	GAL. 4
12.	PROV. 21, 22	2 COR. 4	27.	ISAIAH 10, 11, 12	GAL. 5
13.	PROV. 23, 24	2 COR. 5	28.	ISAIAH 13, 14, 15	GAL. 6
14.	PROV. 25, 26, 27	2 COR. 6	29.	ISAIAH 16, 17, 18	EPH. 1
15.	PROV. 28, 29	2 COR. 7	30.	ISAIAH 19, 20, 21	EPH. 2

OCTOBER

	Morning	*Evening*		*Morning*	*Evening*
1.	ISAIAH 22, 23	EPH. 3	17.	ISAIAH 62, 63, 64	1 THESS. 5
2.	ISAIAH 24, 25, 26	EPH. 4	18.	ISAIAH 65, 66	2 THESS. 1
3.	ISAIAH 27, 28	EPH. 5	19.	JER. 1, 2	2 THESS. 2
4.	ISAIAH 29, 30	EPH. 6	20.	JER. 3, 4	2 THESS. 3
5.	ISAIAH 31, 32, 33	PHIL. 1	21.	JER. 5, 6	1 TIM. 1
6.	ISAIAH 34, 35, 36	PHIL. 2	22.	JER. 7, 8	1 TIM. 2
7.	ISAIAH 37, 38	PHIL. 3	23.	JER. 9, 10	1 TIM. 3
8.	ISAIAH 39, 40	PHIL. 4	24.	JER. 11, 12, 13	1 TIM. 4
9.	ISAIAH 41, 42	COL. 1	25.	JER. 14, 15, 16	1 TIM. 5
10.	ISAIAH 43, 44	COL. 2	26.	JER. 17, 18, 19	1 TIM. 6
11.	ISAIAH 45, 46, 47	COL. 3	27.	JER. 20, 21, 22	2 TIM. 1
12.	ISAIAH 48, 49	COL. 4	28.	JER. 23, 24	2 TIM. 2
13.	ISAIAH 50, 51, 52	1 THESS. 1	29.	JER. 25, 26	2 TIM. 3
14.	ISAIAH 53, 54, 55	1 THESS. 2	30.	JER. 27, 28	2 TIM. 4
15.	ISAIAH 56, 57, 58	1 THESS. 3	31.	JER. 29, 30	TITUS 1
16.	ISAIAH 59, 60, 61	1 THESS. 4			

NOVEMBER

	Morning	Evening		Morning	Evening
1.	JER. 31, 32	TITUS 2	16.	EZEK. 13, 14, 15	HEB. 11:20–40
2.	JER. 33, 34, 35	TITUS 3	17.	EZEK. 16	HEB. 12
3.	JER. 36, 37	PHILEMON	18.	EZEK. 17, 18, 19	HEB. 13
4.	JER. 38, 39	HEB. 1	19.	EZEK. 20, 21	JAMES 1
5.	JER. 40, 41, 42	HEB. 2	20.	EZEK. 22, 23	JAMES 2
6.	JER. 43, 44, 45	HEB. 3	21.	EZEK. 24, 25, 26	JAMES 3
7.	JER. 46, 47, 48	HEB. 4	22.	EZEK. 27, 28	JAMES 4
8.	JER. 49, 50	HEB. 5	23.	EZEK. 29, 30, 31	JAMES 5
9.	JER. 51, 52	HEB. 6	24.	EZEK. 32, 33	1 PETER 1
10.	LAM. 1, 2	HEB. 7	25.	EZEK. 34, 35	1 PETER 2
11.	LAM. 3, 4, 5	HEB. 8	26.	EZEK. 36, 37	1 PETER 3
12.	EZEK. 1, 2, 3	HEB. 9	27.	EZEK. 38, 39	1 PETER 4
13.	EZEK. 4, 5, 6	HEB. 10:1–23	28.	EZEK. 40	1 PETER 5
14.	EZEK. 7, 8, 9	HEB. 10:24–39	29.	EZEK. 41, 42	2 PETER 1
15.	EZEK. 10, 11, 12	HEB. 11:1–19	30.	EZEK. 43, 44	2 PETER 2

DECEMBER

	Morning	Evening		Morning	Evening
1.	EZEK. 45, 46	2 PETER 3	17.	OBADIAH	REV. 8
2.	EZEK. 47, 48	1 JOHN 1	18.	JONAH	REV. 9
3.	DAN. 1, 2	1 JOHN 2	19.	MICAH 1, 2, 3	REV. 10
4.	DAN. 3, 4	1 JOHN 3	20.	MICAH 4, 5	REV. 11
5.	DAN. 5, 6	1 JOHN 4	21.	MICAH 6, 7	REV. 12
6.	DAN. 7, 8	1 JOHN 5	22.	NAHUM	REV. 13
7.	DAN. 9, 10	2 JOHN	23.	HABAKKUK	REV. 14
8.	DAN. 11, 12	3 JOHN	24.	ZEPHANIAH	REV. 15
9.	HOSEA 1–4	JUDE	25.	HAGGAI	REV. 16
10.	HOSEA 5–8	REV. 1	26.	ZECH. 1, 2, 3	REV. 17
11.	HOSEA 9, 10, 11	REV. 2	27.	ZECH. 4, 5, 6	REV. 18
12.	HOSEA 12, 13, 14	REV. 3	28.	ZECH. 7, 8, 9	REV. 19
13.	JOEL	REV. 4	29.	ZECH. 10, 11, 12	REV. 20
14.	AMOS 1, 2, 3	REV. 5	30.	ZECH. 13, 14	REV. 21
15.	AMOS 4, 5, 6	REV. 6	31.	MALACHI	REV. 22
16.	AMOS 7, 8, 9	REV. 7			

Appendix C
Recommended Reading List

Titles, Authors, and Publishers

Section 1

	Title	Author	Publisher
1.	*The Genesis Question*	Hugh Ross	NavPress
2.	*The Sovereignty of God*	Arthur W. Pink	Baker
3.	*The Hand of God*	Alistair Begg	Moody
4.	*God: Discover His Character*	Bill Bright	New Life
5.	*The Names of Christ*	T. C. Horton and Charles E. Hurlburt	Moody
6.	*Two Cities, Two Loves*	James Montgomery Boice	InterVarsity
7.	*Angels: Elect and Evil*	C. Fred Dickason	Moody

Section 2

	Title	Author	Publisher
8.	*Discovering God's Will*	Sinclair B. Ferguson	Banner of Truth
9.	*Romans 1–8* (MNTC)	John MacArthur, Jr.	Moody
10.	*For God So Loved*	J. Sidlow Baxter	Kregel
11.	*The Atonement*	Leon Morris	InterVarsity
12.	*The Heart of Christianity*	Ron Rhodes	Harvest
13.	*Hope: The Heart's Great Quest*	David Ackman	Vine

Section 3

	Title	Author	Publisher
14.	*The Way of Life*	Charles Hodge	Banner of Truth
15.	*Faith Alone*	R. C. Sproul	Baker
16.	*Knowing God*	J. I. Packer	InterVarsity

Title	Author	Publisher
17. *I Really Want to Change . . . So, Help Me God*	James MacDonald	Moody
18. *The Last Things*	Paul Helm	Banner of Truth
19. *How You Can Be Sure That You Will Spend Eternity with God*	Erwin W. Lutzer	Moody

Section 4

Title	Author	Publisher
20. *Loving God*	Chuck Colson	Zondervan
21. *Building Up One Another*	Gene Getz	Chariot Victor
22. *A Heart for God*	Sinclair B. Ferguson	NavPress
23. *Fasting for Spiritual Breakthrough*	Elmer L. Towns	Regal
24. *A Christmas Carol*	Charles Dickens	Various publishers
25. *How to Pray in the Spirit*	John Bunyan	Kregel
26. *The Lost Art of Disciple Making*	Leroy Eims	Zondervan

Section 5

Title	Author	Publisher
27. *The Joy of Fearing God*	Jerry Bridges	WaterBrook
28. *The Beginnings*	Paul Helm	Banner of Truth
29. *God in the Wasteland*	David F. Wells	Eerdmans
30. *Personal Holiness in Times of Temptation*	Bruce H. Wilkinson	Harvest
31. *Financial Freedom*	Ray Linder	Moody
32. *Not Good If Detached*	Corrie ten Boom	Fleming H. Revell
33. *The Other Side of Love*	Gary Chapman	Moody

Section 6

Title	Author	Publisher
34. *Something New Under the Sun*	Ray Pritchard	Moody

Title	Author	Publisher
35. *Been There. Done That. Now What?*	Ed Young	Broadman & Holman
36. *The Shorter Catechism with Scripture Proofs*		Banner of Truth
37. *Alive for the First Time*	David C. Needham	Multnomah
38. *The Forgotten Blessing*	Henry Holloman	Word
39. *He Gave Gifts*	Charles R. Swindoll	Insights for Living

Section 7

Title	Author	Publisher
40. *The Glorious Pursuit*	Gary L. Thomas	NavPress
41. *When Good Men Are Tempted*	Bill Perkins	Zondervan
42. *The Pillars of Christian Character*	John F. MacArthur	Crossway
43. *The Weight of Your Words*	Joseph M. Stowell	Moody
44. *Loving God with All Your Mind*	Elizabeth George	Harvest
45. *Our Covenant God*	Kay Arthur	WaterBrook Press
46. *Keeping the Heart*	John Flavel	Soli Deo Gloria

Section 8

Title	Author	Publisher
47. *A Passion for Souls*	Lyle W. Dorsett	Moody
48. *As Iron Sharpens Iron*	Howard and William Hendricks	Moody
49. *Finding Common Ground*	Tim Downs	Moody
50. *The Life You've Always Wanted*	John Ortberg	Zondervan
51. *Kingdom Life in a Fallen World*	Sinclair B. Ferguson	NavPress
52. *Life Essentials*	William L. Thrasher, Jr. (General Editor)	Moody

Appendix D
Scripture Verses by Topic

Section 1

	Topic	Book of the Bible	Translation
1.	God's Creation	Psalm 111:2	NKJV
2.	God's Sovereignty	1 Chronicles 29:11	NKJV
3.	Providence	Isaiah 46:9–10	NLT
4.	God's Knowledge	Romans 11:33–36	NLT
5.	Names and Titles of Jesus	Philippians 2:9–11	NLT
6.	Truth	Matthew 13:10–13	NLT
7.	Angels	Revelation 5:11–12	NLT

Section 2

	Topic	Book of the Bible	Translation
8.	Knowing God's Plan	Isaiah 55:8–11	NLT
9.	God's Wrath	Romans 1:18	NASB
10.	God's Love	John 3:16	NKJV
11.	The Atonement	Isaiah 53:5–6	NKJV
12.	Salvation	Ephesians 2:8–9	NLT
13.	Hope	Hebrews 10:23	NLT

Section 3

	Topic	Book of the Bible	Translation
14.	Faith and Repentance	Acts 2:37–38	NIV
15.	Justification	Acts 13:39	NKJV
16.	Adoption	Romans 8:14–17	NKJV
17.	Sanctification	Galatians 2:20	KJV
18.	Glorification	1 Corinthians 15:42–44	NLT
19.	Assurance	John 10:27–29	NLT

Section 4

	Topic	Book of the Bible	Translation
20.	Loving God	Matthew 25:35–40	NLT
21.	Fellowship	Philippians 2:2–4	NLT
22.	Submission	1 Peter 5:5	NKJV
23.	Fasting	Isaiah 58:6–8	NLT
24.	Compassion	Zechariah 7:9–10	NLT
25.	Effective Prayer	Jeremiah 33:3	NASB
26.	Discipleship	Matthew 28:19–20	NLT

Section 5

	Topic	Book of the Bible	Translation
27.	The Fear of God	1 Peter 1:17	NLT
28.	Deceptive Faith	Matthew 7:21	NLT
29.	Idolatry	Deuteronomy 11:16	NKJV
30.	Worldliness	1 John 2:15	KJV
31.	Materialism	Luke 12:15	RSV
32.	Temptation	1 Corinthians 10:13	RSV
33.	Anger	Ephesians 4:26–27	NIV

Section 6

	Topic	Book of the Bible	Translation
34.	Common Sense	Proverbs 10:21	NLT
35.	Setting Priorities	Luke 10:39–42	NKJV
36.	Success	Matthew 22:37–39	NIV
37.	Practice	Philippians 3:13–14	NIV
38.	Self-Control and Endurance	2 Peter 1:6	NLT
39.	Spiritual Gifts	1 Timothy 4:14	NASB

Section 7

	Topic	Book of the Bible	Translation
40.	What We Hear	Acts 24:16	NIV
41.	What We See	Mark 9:47	NLT
42.	What We Read	Romans 12:2	RSV
43.	What We Say	James 3:2	NLT
44.	What We Think	1 Samuel 16:7	NLT
45.	What We Do	James 2:14	NLT
46.	What We Are	Proverbs 4:23	NKJV

Section 8

	Topic	Book of the Bible	Translation
47.	Heroes	Hebrews 11:32–34	NIV
48.	Mentoring	2 Timothy 2:2	NLT
49.	Reproducing	Colossians 4:5–6	NLT
50.	Trustworthiness	Daniel 6:4	NIV
51.	Character	Psalm 1:1–3	RSV
52.	Godliness	2 Peter 3:11–12	NIV

Moody Press, a ministry of Moody Bible Institute,
is designed for education, evangelization, and edification.
If we may assist you in knowing more about Christ
and the Christian life, please write us without obligation:
Moody Press, c/o MLM, Chicago, Illinois 60610.